All the Ordinary Angels

Nick Leather is currently Playwright-in-Residence at Manchester's Royal Exchange Theatre, having won a Pearson Playwrights' Bursary for his play *Drinks with Sammy Baloo*, and is an Associate Writer of the Liverpool Everyman and Playhouse. He had previously won a New Playwrights Award for the Royal Exchange and a Development Award from the BBC, and is both a BBC Drama Sparks Writer and a graduate of the Royal Court Young Writers Programme. *All the Ordinary Angels* won the Pearson Best Play Award 2004.

Nick Leather

All the Ordinary Angels

B L O O M S B U R Y

LONDON • NEW DELHI • NEW YORK • SYDNEY

Bloomsbury Methuen Drama

An imprint of Bloomsbury Publishing Plc

50 Bedford Square   1385 Broadway
London   New York
WC1B 3DP   NY 10018
UK   USA

www.bloomsbury.com

Bloomsbury is a registered trade mark of Bloomsbury Publishing Plc

First published in 2005 by Methuen Publishing Ltd

© 2005 Nick Leather

Visit www.bloomsbury.com to find out more about our authors and their books
You will find extracts, author interviews, author events and you can sign up for newsletters to be the first to hear about our latest releases and special offers.

British Library Cataloguing-in-Publication Data
A catalogue record for this book is available from the British Library.

ISBN: PB: 978-0-4137-7551-1
ePDF: 978-1-4725-3693-8
ePUB: 978-1-4725-3692-1

Library of Congress Cataloging-in-Publication Data
A catalog record for this book is available from the Library of Congress.

for

me mum, me dad

our gill, our vics

+

my joanna

X

With special thanks to

the Pearson Playwrights' Scheme,
for giving me the chance to write this play
and The Royal Exchange Theatre
for being my home.

All the Ordinary Angels received its world premiere at the Royal Exchange Theatre, Manchester, on 26 October 2005. The cast was as follows:

Giuseppe	Peter Polycarpou
Rocco	Craig Cheetham
Bernie	Sarah Ball
Lino	Al Weaver
Lulu	Lucy Gaskell

Director	Michael Buffong
Set Designer	Es Devlin
Costumes	Emma Williams
Lighting Designer	Johanna Town
Sound Designer	Steve Brown
Dialect Coach	Mark Langley
Company Manager	Katie Vine
Stage Manager	Francis Lynch
Deputy Stage Manager	Anne Baxter
Assistant Stage Manager	Marisa Ferguson

All the Ordinary Angels

'We'll go on to midnight if necessary
to serve all these good people'

G. Godden
Operations Manager for the first Soviet McDonald's
on its opening night in Moscow, February 1990

Characters

Giuseppe, *a man in his early sixties*
Rocco, *a man in his late thirties*
Bernie, *a woman in her late thirties*
Lino, *a boy in his late twenties*
Lulu, *a girl in her early twenties*

Note on the Text

A / in dialogue indicates a point of interruption

Act One

One

Mid-November 1989. Storage area of Raffa's ice-cream factory, Manchester.

It's dark. A number of boxes – some wooden, some cardboard – are half-scattered and half-stacked on the factory floor. Each of them has 'Raffa's Ices' stamped on the side. A girl jumps up onto one of the wooden boxes, then steps from box to box. She's dressed in office clothes and wears a thin pair of gloves on her hands. She stops on the box in the middle and spins round. Suddenly, an unseen voice speaks:

Lino (*in box*) Hello.

Stunned, **Lulu** *stops spinning and falls off the box.*

Lulu Who said that?

Lino (*in box*) Me.

Lulu Where are yer?

Lino (*in box*) In 'ere.

Lulu In where?

Lino *bangs and kicks his box so that it rocks.* **Lulu** *moves over to it.*

Lulu What yer doin' in a box?

Lino (*in box*) Me brother. He put me in.

Lulu Why?

Lino (*in box*) It's me birthday.

Lulu And his pressie to you . . . is you? (*Beat.*) That what you asked for?

Lino (*in box*) Not what I asked for at all.

Lulu How're you gonna unwrap yourself?

Lino (*in box*) I – I can't. Need you to help me.

Lulu   I should phone the police.

Lino (*in box*)   What about?

Lulu   About you.

Lino (*in box*)   Me?

Lulu   Breakin' in.

Lino (*in box*)   To a box?

Lulu   No.

Lino (*in box*)   I've been tryna break out.

Lulu   The buildin', not the box.

Lino (*in box*)   I didn't.

Lulu   You've hid in a box. To get in a buildin'. To steal the ice cream.

Lino (*in box*)   Don't need to. Work 'ere.

Lulu   You don't. I do.

Lino (*in box*)   And I do too.

Lulu   Prove it.

Lino (*in box*)   How?

Lulu   I've got keys. Have you got keys?

Lino (*in box*)   How do I know you've got keys?

Lulu *pulls out a set of keys and holds them up over* **Lino**'s *box.*

Lulu   See?

Lino (*in box*)   No. I don't.

Lulu *rattles her keys.*

Lulu   Hear?

Lino (*in box*)   Sounds like an 'andful o' money.

Lulu   Well, you rattle your keys.

Lino (*in box*)   I – I 'aven't got 'em on me.

Lulu   Ha!

Lino (*in box*)   'Aven't got anythin' on me.

Lulu   Anythin' at all?

Lino (*in box*)   Nope.

Lulu   Pervert. I'm deffo callin' the police.

Lino (*in box*)   Good. Maybe they'll get me out.

Lulu   You oughta be locked up.

Lino (*in box*)   I am.

Lulu   I'm gonna phone 'em then.

Lino (*in box*)   Will you tell 'em it's my factory?

Lulu   But it isn't.

Lino (*in box*)   It is. I run the factory. Rocco runs the office. Papa runs the business.

Lulu *pauses for a moment, sitting down on a box.*

Lulu   It's not . . . you're not . . . Merlino?

Lino (*in box*)   Lino, yeah.

Lulu   I am *so* sorry.

Lino (*in box*)   It's alright.

Lulu   I didn't recognise yer.

Lino (*in box*)   That's understandable.

Lulu   So Rocco's locked yer in a box? For your birthday?

Lino (*in box*)   He did it last year 'n' all. I didn't find it funny then either.

Lulu   I'll get you out.

*She starts to search around the factory for something to get **Lino** out of his box.*

Lulu I'm helpin' out in the office.

Lino (*in box*) I know.

Lulu You do?

Lino (*in box*) You're Louise, aren't yer?

Lulu Everyone calls me Lulu.

Lino (*in box*) I didn't think we needed helpin' out.

Lulu Well, your dad must think you do.

Lino (*in box*) How come you're still 'ere?

Lulu Rocco left me to lock up. (*Beat.*) Will he be comin' back?

Lino (*in box*) Didn't last year. And when Papa let me out in the mornin', he had a go at me for eatin' all the wafers. (*Beat.*) I only did it to make more room.

Lulu *spots the emergency fire-axe on the wall and walks towards it.*

Lulu Yer gonna get rid o' me? (*Beat.*) Never stay anywhere for very long. (*Beat.*) Was hopin' to make the second day, though.

Lino (*in box*) Couldn't sack you if I wanted to.

Lulu So you do want to?

Lino (*in box*) I don't know: jus' know I wanna get out.

Lulu *pulls the axe from its mount. Immediately a fire alarm starts to go off and a bright red light starts to flash.*

Lino (*in box*) Is there a fire?

Lulu No.

Lino (*in box*) One o' the tanks is gas. And it leaks!

Lulu There isn't a fire.

Lino (*in box*) We're gonna be blown into a million pieces!

Lino's *box rocks frantically as tries to kick his way from the inside out.*

Lulu   Only took the axe from the wall!

Lino (*in box*)   That sets the fire alarm off!

Lulu   I know that now!

Lino (*in box*)   Get me out!

Lulu   Should I just hit it, then?

Lino (*in box*)   Hard as you can!

Lulu   Watch out!

Lulu *hits the box with the axe till there's a hole in the top of it, then runs and puts the axe back on its mount. The alarm stops ringing, but the red light continues to flash. From up on the roof outside, the sound of wings flapping can be heard. One of* **Lino***'s hands shoots out of the hole in the box and offers itself to* **Lulu**.

Lino (*in box*)   Pleased to − pleased to meet you.

Lulu   Why've you got goo on your hands?

Lino (*in box*)   Rocco egged me. And floured me.

Lulu   He didn't.

Lino (*in box*)   He did.

Lulu   Oh.

Lino (*in box*)   Why've you got gloves on?

Lulu   Always wear gloves.

Lino (*in box*)   Do you?

Lulu   I do.

Lino (*in box*)   Right.

Lulu *pulls at the bits of wood around the hole in the top of the box, whilst* **Lino** *pushes them from the inside. As soon as the hole is big enough, his head appears − covered in eggs and flour.*

Lino   Hiya.

Lulu   Hey.

Lino *smiles nervously. The sounds of wings flapping continues to come from the roof.*

Lulu   When I was a kid and I heard your van outside, I could never get me shoes on quick enough. Always had a cornet in each hand. (*Beat.*) Me dad used to say I'd end up lookin' like ice cream if I wasn't careful.

Lino   Well, you do a bit. Jus' tryna work out which flavour.

Lulu   You can't look like a flavour.

Lino   You do.

Lulu *looks up in the direction of the flapping wings.*

Lulu   What *is* that?

Lino   There's hundreds o' birds nest on the roof. That's why it rains in.

Lulu   Sounds like the whole factory's gonna fly away.

Lino   Feels like it, too.

Pause.

Lulu   Soz.

Lino   For what?

Lulu   For sayin' I'd call the police.

Lino   No probs.

Lulu   Comin' out, then?

Lino   No.

Lulu   Why not?

Lino   Got no clothes on.

Lulu   Oh yeah. Want me jacket?

Lino   I'll get eggs on it. And flour.

Lulu   Don't matter.

Lino   Don't it?

Lulu No.

She takes her jacket off and lays it next to the box.

How're yer gettin' home?

Lino On me bike.

Lulu Yer can't ride home like that. (*Beat.*) I'll give yer a lift.

Lino Right. Yeah. Thanks.

Lulu I'll wait outside for yer then.

Lulu *goes to exit but, as she turns,* **Lino** *speaks.*

Lino I couldn't sack yer.

Lulu Yer said.

Lino But if I could . . .

Lulu Yeah?

Lino I wouldn't want to.

Lulu *pauses as* **Lino** *disappears back into the box. He breaks more of the wood above him, before his head reappears. This time he forces his hands and arms through too – all covered in eggs, flour and bits of ice-cream wafer.*

Lulu Lino?

Lino What?

Lulu Happy birthday then.

Lino Eh?

Lulu Happy birthday.

She exits. **Lino** *breaks completely out of the box, lit by the red light.*

Two

Continuous. Living room of **Bernie** *and* **Rocco Raffa***'s house, Manchester.*

A sheet of tarpaulin has been folded over to cover something up. Standing over it is a man in a black suit, with white shirt and black pencil-tie. His collar is undone, his tie is loose, and a cigarette hangs from his top lip. This is **Rocco Raffa**. *He holds a sledgehammer one-handed and stares at the mound in the middle of the tarpaulin for a second before lifting the hammer high up above his head with both hands. Just as he's about to bring it crashing down on the mound a woman runs in, carrying two shopping bags, and looking distressed. This is* **Bernie**. *Her speech is always aided – and occasionally replaced entirely – by hand-gestures.*

Bernie What's happened?

Taken by surprise, **Rocco** *drops the hammer over his shoulder and lurches around.*

Rocco What?!

Bernie The accident! There's been a – (*mimes 'car crash'*).

Rocco Where?

Bernie *points to the front of the house.*

Rocco Is my car alright?

Bernie Are *you* alright?

Rocco Yer can see I'm alright – but my car –

Bernie It's not *your* car –

Rocco Then whose car?

Bernie I didn't actually *see* the car.

Rocco Either o' the cars?

Bernie No.

Rocco Ambulance?

Bernie *shakes her head.*

Rocco   So how d'yer know there's been a bloody accident?

Bernie   The wall – the front wall – it's – (*mimes 'gone'*).

Rocco   The wall?

Bernie   Yeah.

Rocco   Is that all?

Bernie   Yer should see it.

Rocco   I 'ave seen it. (*Beat.*) I did it.

Bernie   You had the accident?

Rocco   There 'asn't been a bloody accident.

He picks up the sledgehammer from the floor. **Bernie** *looks confused.*

Rocco   I knocked it down.

Bernie   You've demolished our garden wall?

Rocco *nods.* **Bernie** *drops her shopping bags and pulls* **Rocco***'s cigarette from his mouth.*

Rocco   I'm smokin' that!

Bernie   Not in here you're not. Now what've you done with it?

Rocco   With what?

Bernie   The wall!

Rocco *turns round and pulls back the tarpaulin to reveal the wall. He stands at the other side of it from* **Bernie**.

Bernie   You've brought our garden wall into the living room?

Rocco   I'm breakin' it up.

Bernie   In the *living* room?

Rocco   They're knockin' the Berlin Wall down.

Bernie   And what's this? A tribute?

Rocco   Sort of. Guess what's in it for Rocco?

Bernie   I have no idea.

Rocco   I'm gonna sell it.

Bernie   The garden wall?

Rocco   Pieces of it.

Bernie *takes a puff of* **Rocco***'s cigarette as he pulls the tarpaulin back over the wall, before thumping it with the sledgehammer. Reaching beneath the tarpaulin, he pulls out a solitary brick.*

Rocco   It's history. Instant history. And punters pay for history.

Bernie   So?

Rocco   So I'll give 'em what they want.

Bernie   What? What are you giving them?

Rocco *throws the stone to* **Bernie**.

Rocco   I'm sellin' em . . . the bricks.

Bernie   Which bricks?

Rocco   These bricks. These pieces of history.

Bernie   That's not history. That's our garden wall.

Rocco   It's *our* history.

Bernie   It's not the Berlin Wall. It's not world bloody history.

Rocco   Might as well be. What's the difference? Bricks is bricks.

Bernie   You're gonna pretend these bricks are sommat they're not and sell them off at fifty pence a pop?

Rocco   Fifty pee? This is the bastard Berlin Wall. Worth a fiver each at least.

Bernie   It's not the Berlin Wall, it's *our* wall!

She throws the stone back to **Rocco**.

Rocco Folk buy footie shirts for their kids, right? Pay top whack for 'em. An' their kids are like, 'Yeah! I've got a United shirt'. But 'ave they? 'Ave they got the actual shirt that Bryan Robson wears? 'Ave they bollocks. They're replicas. Not real. Replica. Not really United. But the next best thing.

Bernie So when you sell it you're gonna tell people it's Replica Berlin Wall, not Actual Berlin Wall?

Rocco What papa ever told his bambino – on Chrimbo mornin' – that the shirt he'd just unwrapped, just put on, wa'n't real – it was replica. What papa ever said that? (*Beat.*) You let 'em live the dream.

Bernie But people aren't kids.

Rocco I can't see any difference. An' if people wanna believe somethin', Rocco sez let 'em believe.

Bernie Wish I believed sommat. (*Beat.*) I mean, it *is* sort of inspiring.

Rocco What?

Bernie The Wall comin' down.

Rocco Knew you'd come round.

Bernie Not *this* one! *That* one!

Rocco *Which* one?

Bernie The *Berlin* one!

Rocco Oh.

Bernie This one? As if.

Rocco OK.

Bernie There was a protest on this afternoon. Loads o' people in Albert Square. All against the Poll Tax. All believin' in sommat.

Rocco That's not believin'. That's jus' moanin'.

Bernie We *need* a garden wall, Rocco. We had one. And it's gone.

Rocco That's the beauty of it: with the money we get from sellin' these bricks, we'll be able to build a new wall –

Bernie There was nothin' wrong with the old wall –

Rocco A bigger wall, a better wall –

Bernie I liked the *old* wall.

Rocco It's gone.

Bernie I want it back.

Rocco We can 'ave railin's. Wi' spikes on 'em.

Bernie *takes a long drag of* **Rocco***'s cigarette.*

Bernie And you said you'd given up.

Rocco I 'ave.

Bernie You were puffin' away when I came in.

Rocco You're puffin' away now.

Bernie I'm under stress. There's a wall in the middle of our living room. And it kinda gets in the way.

Rocco Could stick it in the middle o' the bedroom. Might not get in the way there.

Bernie *stubs the cigarette out.*

Bernie Why aren't you at work?

Rocco Left the new girl to lock up.

Bernie On her first day?

Rocco I'm fast-trackin' her.

Bernie You don't even need anyone.

Rocco Was Papa's idea. Not mine.

Bernie Why didn't he ask me? I coulda done it.

Rocco You wouldn't've 'ad the time.

Bernie I would.

Rocco You wouldn't.

Bernie I *would*.

Rocco OK.

Bernie (*beat*) When are we goin' round?

Rocco Where?

Bernie To Giuseppe's. For Lino's birthday.

Rocco We're not.

Bernie Why not?

Rocco Lino can't make it.

Bernie To his own birthday?

Rocco He's goin' out. Gone out. Be out all night.

Bernie He never goes out. Who's he gone out with?

Rocco With friends.

Bernie He hasn't got any friends!

Rocco Well, I don't know!

Bernie I've got cake for him.

Rocco *We* can eat it.

Bernie It's got candles.

Rocco *I'll* blow 'em out.

Bernie You can't blow 'em out! It's not your birthday!

Rocco Now *you're* jus' moanin'.

Bernie I'm not *moaning*, I'm *protesting*.

Rocco Since when did you protest?

Bernie   Since now. Put the wall back up, Rocco.

Rocco   I'm gonna break it apart.

Bernie   Keep it together. Rebuild it.

Rocco *stares at the stone in his hands.* **Bernie** *puts her hands on his and holds them tightly.*

Bernie   Used to love watchin' you. Down by the canal. With all the other lads.

Rocco   Rocco Raffa was always the best at skimmers. *Always* won.

Bernie   I know. You won me.

Rocco (*beat*)   You want me to rebuild it?

Bernie   I could help you. We could rebuild it together.

Rocco   Rocco Raffa doesn't need help.

Bernie   So you will?

Rocco   I might.

Bernie   You might?

Rocco (*beat*)   I will.

Three

Christmas Eve 1989. Dining room of Giuseppe Raffa's house, Manchester.

Religious iconography surrounds the dining table at which the family sit. At the head of the table, in a chair like a throne, sits an immaculately turned out man: his grey hair slicked back beneath a paper crown and his thin moustache well-groomed. This is **Giuseppe Raffa**. *At one side of the table sits* **Rocco** *and at the other* **Lino**. *At the far-end sits* **Bernie**. *Half-empty plates and Christmas crackers litter the table.*

Giuseppe   Hands together. Eyes closed.

He puts his hands together and closes his eyes. **Lino** *and* **Bernie**
follow suit. There is a pause, then **Giuseppe** *reopens his eyes.*

Giuseppe   Rocco: you might not come to mass with rest of
us, but you can still bow your head when you're round my
table.

Bernie *opens her eyes, mimes at* **Rocco** *to close his, then closes hers
again.* **Giuseppe** *stares at* **Rocco** *for a moment.* **Rocco** *finally
closes his eyes and* **Giuseppe** *follows suit.*

Giuseppe   Almighty God, as we celebrate feast of seven
fishes this Christmas Eve – may we offer our thanks for year
that's passed and ask that you continue to guide us in special
year to come – as I retire.

Rocco   Retire?

Bernie   Rocco!

Giuseppe   Forty-four years of gelato, and it's finally time
for Giuseppe Raffa to come in from cold.

Rocco   You're really retirin'?

Lino   Papa?

Giuseppe *keeps his eyes closed and his hands together. After a pause,*
Bernie *closes her eyes again, then* **Lino** *does too.* **Rocco** *stares at*
Giuseppe, *and slowly starts to smile.*

Giuseppe   Bless this family. And bless our gelato. (*Beat.*)
May we always rejoice in your goodness. Through Christ,
our Lord. Amen.

Bernie *and* **Lino** (*in unison*)   Amen.

Giuseppe, **Bernie** *and* **Lino** *open their eyes and look at* **Rocco**.
There is a pause, then:

Rocco   A-*men.*

Bernie   Giuseppe?

Giuseppe *stands up, straightens the paper crown on his head, and
speaks:*

Giuseppe   When Nonno Raffa returned from Canada at end of war, he no longer had stomach for gelato. So he passed biz down to me. Now I do same: to you.

Bernie   Always thought you'd go on for ever.

Giuseppe   I made Raffa's Ices great. And it needs to be great again. But I can't sit in van, with hatch closed and rain beating down on roof, any longer. (*Beat.*) All my life I've looked after my family. Now it's time for my family to look after me.

He starts to circle the table.

Rocco   So the business is mine? Raffa's Ices is all Rocco's?

Bernie   And Lino's.

Rocco   *His?*

Bernie   Well, *ours*. We can all help out. I can – (*mimes 'help'.*)

Giuseppe   Only one person can run biz.

Rocco   Exactly.

Bernie   So it *is* Rocco's?

Giuseppe *places the palm of his right hand on* **Rocco***'s head as he passes him.*

Giuseppe   Rocco – you can't run factory. You're no good at making gelato.

Lino   It's mine?!

Rocco   Papa!

Giuseppe *places the palm of his right hand on* **Lino***'s head as he passes him.*

Giuseppe   Merlino – you can't run office. You're no good at making money.

Bernie   Then – (*mimes 'who'*)?

Giuseppe   One will have to learn. I stood up to be counted once, now you must do same. (*Beat.*) Stand up.

Rocco *and* **Bernie** *stand up.*

Giuseppe   Not you, Bernadette.

Bernie *sits down again.* **Giuseppe** *glares at* **Lino***.*

Lino   Me?

Lino *stands up.* **Giuseppe** *returns to the head of the table.*

Bernie   Giuseppe, I / don't . . .

Giuseppe *claps his hands together twice.* **Bernie** *is silenced.*

Giuseppe   For twelve months, everything will be split.
Rocco, Merlino – you'll be in competition with one another.
Set of tanks each, and our regular customers, orders and
routes divided between you. But what you do with, and on
top of them, is up to you.

Lino   What about Lulu?

Rocco   Sack her. She's useless.

Lino   She ain't.

Rocco   Is.

Lino   Can't sack her.

Bernie   Lino's sweet on her.

Lino   Am not.

Giuseppe   She'll be split between you, too. She'll work
with you both.

Bernie   Is that why you got someone else in? Cos you
knew you were (*mimes 'going'*)?

Giuseppe   And in autumn next year – on what would've
been your mamma's birthday – I'll take your accounts, I'll
look – and one who has sold most ice cream . . . will win.

Rocco   Win what, Papa? What's in it for Rocco?

Giuseppe   Win biz. Raffa's Ices will be theirs.

Bernie   And what about the other one?

Giuseppe *shrugs, then smiles.*

Rocco   So what are yer sayin'?

Giuseppe (*laughs*)   Don't lose.

Lino   But if I'm in the factory and Rocco's in the office how / do . . .

Giuseppe   You'll both be in factory. You'll both be in office. You'll both be in street. In vans.

Rocco   You want me to make the stuff? Actually make it?

Lino   Paperwork an' orderin'? Am rubbish at all that.

Giuseppe   One will learn. One will have to learn. That one will win. (*Beat.*) And fate of loser lies not with me – but with winner.

Bernie   You can't pit one son against the other.

Rocco   It should come to me. Should be Rocco's.

Lino   Give it to him, Papa. I don't wanna run the business – jus' wanna make ice cream.

Bernie   Share it. Share the business – (*mimes 'between us all'*).

Giuseppe   Raffa's Ices needs leader. It's biz, not charity.

Rocco   He knows he can't sell the stuff, Papa. So give it to me.

Giuseppe   You think you're right person, Rocco?

Rocco   I know I am.

Giuseppe   Then prove it. Earn it. Fight to win.

Bernie *stands up too.*

Bernie   You want the blood of your own children?

Rocco   Bernie!

Giuseppe   I want to be father of fighters!

Bernie   But it's not about /

Giuseppe *claps his hands together twice again.*

Giuseppe   Bernadette, when did you / start . . .

Rocco   She's always moanin' / at the . . .

Bernie   I'm protestin'.

Giuseppe   *Sit.*

Rocco *and* **Lino** *sit down.* **Bernie** *remains standing.*

Bernie   Don't wanna sit down any more.

Giuseppe, **Rocco** *and* **Lino** *all stare at* **Bernie**. *There is a pause, then she sits down.* **Giuseppe** *takes the paper crown from his head, scrunches it up into a ball in the palm of his hand and drops it onto the table before also sitting down.*

Giuseppe   When war began, they stoned this house. Never ever forget that. We'd been here years, but became enemy overnight. People we knew. Smashed *every* window.

Bernie   We won't forget.

Rocco *(whispers)*   Wish we could.

Giuseppe   Nonno Raffa was snatched from his bed. Taken away. Put on boat. When Ancoats woke up next morning, it was full of families without fathers. *(Beat.)* And when their boat sank – sea swallowed most of them up. But there – in ice-cold water, beneath waves – Nonno Raffa finally learned how to swim. *(Beat.)* And down in basement – as I picked all stones from barrels of gelato – I learned too. Now it's time for you. *(Beat. To* **Bernie**.) So you disagree? *(To* **Rocco**.) And you? *(To* **Lino**.) What about you? I make decisions. It's up to me. Soon – one of you'll make decisions. Who? That's up to you. *(Beat.)* Ragazzi.

Giuseppe *motions to* **Rocco** *and* **Lino**. **Lino** *leans forward and offers his hand to* **Rocco**. **Rocco** *picks up the one remaining unpulled cracker and offers that. They pull it.* **Rocco** *wins, takes the contents from the cracker, and unfolds another paper crown. He puts it on. A clock starts to chime midnight.*

Giuseppe   *Ragazzi.*

Rocco *offers* **Lino** *his hand.* **Lino** *takes it. They shake hands as the clock chimes for a final time, then* **Giuseppe** *motions to* **Bernie**.

Giuseppe   It's new day, prepare meat.

Four

Late February 1990. Tib Lock on the Rochdale Canal – at the rear of the Hacienda nightclub, Manchester.

As **Lino** *and* **Lulu** *exit the club and walk down towards the canal, the music give way to rushing water.* **Lino** *wears a hooded top and baggy trousers, whilst* **Lulu** *is more glammed up and spins round and round.*

Lino   Your brother seemed nice. Dead popular.

Lulu   That's cos o' what he does, not who he is. (*Beat.*) Why don't yer try some?

Lino   Nah.

Lulu   Makes your soul spin.

The rushing of water becomes louder and louder. **Lino** *watches* **Lulu** *as she spins.*

Lino   Already is.

Lulu *spins to the edge of the canal.*

Lino   Careful: don't fall in.

Lulu   S'alright.

Lino   Be freezin' in there.

Lulu   Reckon you could jump it?

Lino   The – the canal?

Lulu   Reckon yer could. Could jump that easy.

Lino   I'm not Superman.

Lulu   I'm not sayin' yer could fly it – jus' jump it.

Lino   Superman di'n't actually fly. Not originally. They were – were just jumps. Really big jumps.

Lulu   I stand corrected.

Lino *peers into the canal.* **Lulu** *nudges him, then grabs him quickly.*

Lulu   Saved your life!

Lino *screams.* **Lulu** *bursts out laughing.*

Lino   Lulu!

Lulu   Was that a scream?

Lino   No. Was a shout.

Lulu   Sounded a lot like a scream.

Lino   Thought I was gonna fall in.

Lulu   I had hold o' yer. Wasn't gonna let go.

She smiles at **Lino**. *He walks towards her, but she turns away – jumping up onto the lock gates, then tiptoeing along them with her arms outstretched.*

Lino   Who's – who's your favourite superhero, then?

Lulu   Don't really know any.

Lino   You do. There's loads. Superman. Spiderman. Loads.

Lulu (*beat*)   Ice-Cream Man.

They smile at each other. **Lino** *starts to hum the* Superman *theme tune, then tries to take his top off. He struggles to get it past his elbows and shoulders, however, and it gets stuck altogether round his head.*

Lulu (*laughs*)   What yer doin'?

Lino *staggers around.* **Lulu** *jumps back down from the gates, takes hold of* **Lino**, *and tries to help him remove his top. Both struggle. When the top does finally come off, they are thrown together – arms round each other – cheek-to-cheek. There is a pause, then – as* **Lino** *goes to kiss her – she turns away from him once more.* **Lino** *watches* *her, then puts the hood on his head and lets the rest of the top hang down his back like a cape. He puts his hand on his hips and strides up to* **Lulu**, *before circling her.*

Lino   Faster than a Mr Whippy. Able to fill small cones with a single scoop.

Lulu   Very good.

Lino   Eh? Eh?

Lulu   You're bein' a superhero?

Lino   Yeah. Yeah.

Lulu (*beat*)   Think yer can beat him?

Lino   Lex Luther?

Lulu   Rocco.

Lino   Oh. (*Beat.*) No.

Lulu   Yeah, yer can.

Lino   I can't, honest.

Lulu   Why can't yer?

Lino   I can't do what he does. I can make stuff that tastes nice, but I – I can't shift it. Rocco musta sold loads more than me in the last few weeks. If someone sez they don't want sommat, I say 'Fair dues' – but he goes on at 'em till they give in. Either convinces folk they want sommat they don't, or they jus' buy it anyway to shut him up.

Lulu   I could help you.

Lino   You do help me. You help both of us.

Lulu   I know I'm meant to be his as much as I'm yours, but I don't have to be – could just help you. And not only with the office stuff – could go out with you in the van 'n' all. Help you sell it.

Lino   Why?

Lulu   It's a game all this, Lino. And I wanna play. (*Beat.*) When I first saw the advert for the job, I thought 'Ice

cream? Smart!' But I never get near it. (*Beat.*) I don't jus'
wanna help in the office – that's borin' – I wanna help in
the factory. Wanna make it. Will you teach me? Will you
show me how?

Lino You want to make the ice cream? *That's* it? That's
why?

Lulu No, that's not why. It's not . . . it's jus' . . .

Lino What?

Lulu Yer should see your face.

Lino When?

Lulu When you're makin' it.

Lino What about it?

Lulu It's like you're . . . paintin'.

Lino Walls?

Lulu Pictures.

Lino Oh.

Lulu It's sweet.

Lino So . . .

Lulu *You're* sweet.

Lino Am I?

Lulu And that's why.

Lino Right.

Lulu *takes a small package from her pocket.*

Lulu Got you a prezzie.

Lino Why?

Lulu You're all 'why's', you!

Lino Well I / mean . . .

Lulu   It's only dead little.

Lino   But no one ever gets me 'owt.

Lulu   Here you go, then.

Lulu *passes the package to* **Lino**. *He rips the wrapping paper off it.*

Lino   Wow! (*Beat.*) What is it?

Lulu   Bubbles. Y'know. That yer blow. Through a thing.

Lino   Oh right. Yeah. Ace.

Lulu   Maybe's I shou'n't've built it up.

Lino   Oh no: they're great. Bubbles.

Lulu   They really *are* great. That's the thing. Yer forget –
when you're older – but they are. They're beautiful.

Lino *shivers as* **Lulu** *takes the small plastic tub from him and jumps
back up onto the lock gates. She flips the cap open, takes the wand out,
and blows a bubble into the air. There is a pause as they watch it fall.*

Lulu   Think you can win, then? Think you can beat
Rocco?

Lino   Maybe. I mean – if they could bring the sea to
Manchester – if they could do that – then yeah, maybe I
can. If you help me. (*Beat.*) Think you can make ice cream?

Lulu   Yeah, maybe I can. If you show me how.

*She blows more bubbles up into the cold night air, and they fall down
onto* **Lino**.

Lino   They *are* beautiful, aren't they?

Lulu   I think – always think that – my hopes 'n' dream 'n'
that – the things I feel inside – that mean somethin' – are
really worth somethin' – that that's them. That that actually
is them. There. Inside the bubbles. Turned into somethin'
proper. Somethin' real.

Lino *steps up onto the lock gates as well and goes to kiss* **Lulu** *once
more – but she leans away to touch one of the bubbles. It bursts. She*

hands **Lino** *the tube, jumps down from the gate, and starts bursting all the bubbles.*

Lino   Shame they have to burst.

He walks down towards the end of the gate, then starts blowing more bubbles up into the air. **Lulu** *looks at him.*

Lulu   I'm gonna help you sell the ice cream.

Lino   And I'm gonna show you how to make it.

He takes a deep breath, then flips the cap shut on the tub and throws it back to **Lulu.** *She catches it, as* **Lino** *prepares to launch himself. At the moment he starts to run,* **Lulu** *shouts:*

Lulu   Stop!

Lino   What?

Lulu   You were gonna, weren't yer? Can't believe you.

Lino   You told me, too.

Lulu   Can you swim?

Lino   I could learn.

Lulu *steps up onto the gate once more – shaking her head as* **Lino** *shrugs, then shivers.*

Lulu   Are yer cold?

Lino   Really really absolutely freezin'.

Lulu (*laughs*)   Put your top on then. You nutter.

Lino *smiles and starts to put his top back on.* **Lulu** *walks down the gate towards him and steadies him as he pulls it over his head. She puts his hood down when his face reappears in it. There is a pause. He kisses her quickly, then steps back – right onto the end of the gate.* **Lulu** *steps forward – also on the end of the gate – alongside him.* **Lino** *licks his lips and nods.*

Lino   Thought so.

Lulu   Eh?

Lino   Vanilla.

Lulu   Vanilla?

Lino   Yeah.

Lulu   Nutter.

Lino   Lulu?

Lulu   What?

Lino (*beat*)   Will you be my Lois Lane?

Five

Good Friday 1990. Paradise Wharf, Manchester.

A Raffa's ice-cream van is parked by the side of the road. The bonnet is raised and steam rises from the engine. **Rocco** *walks towards the van and it explodes. He drops to the ground. Smoke billows from the engine. A mangled version of 'O Sole Mio' plays for a few seconds, before spluttering to a stop as* **Giuseppe** *hurries on and sprays the engine with a fire-extinguisher.*

Giuseppe   Why did you leave engine running?

Rocco   To keep the ice cream cold.

Giuseppe   Look what you've done!

Rocco   Can you fix it?

Giuseppe   I've got to get to mass.

Rocco   Fix the van first.

Giuseppe   It's Good Friday.

Rocco   The freezers'll've cut out now. If the van ain't fixed soon, all the ice cream'll be ruined.

Giuseppe   If you don't start selling more gelato soon, *I'll* be ruined.

Rocco   I can't help it if the factory's fallin' to bits, and the vans keep breakin' down, and the sun never shines.

Giuseppe   There's nothing wrong with factory or vans!

Rocco   It just blew up!

Giuseppe *blasts the engine with the fire extinguisher again.*

Giuseppe   Even Lino's starting to sell.

Rocco   It's not him. It's her.

Giuseppe   She has few months experience. You have years. Gelato is in *your* blood.

Rocco   If I just go / and . . .

Giuseppe   Every night after I first became boss o' biz, I'd go to bed, turn out lamp, close my eyes, and wait for rats to come out. They'd scurry round until . . .

He bangs the fire extinguisher on the ground three times.

Traps got them. And their tails would beat floor. But I wouldn't move. Wouldn't strike match. Wouldn't relight lamp. Just kept my eyes shut tight as they slapped, and cracked, and broke their own backs. Then I'd go to sleep. And sleep well. (*Beat.*) Understand?

Rocco   I'm callin' a garage.

Giuseppe   There'll be no garage called. You don't make money by giving it away.

Rocco   The van *has* to be fixed.

Giuseppe   Just leave it to cool down.

Rocco   But the ice cream'll melt!

Bernie *enters carrying empty plastic bags.*

Rocco (*to* **Bernie**)   What are *you* doin' 'ere?

Bernie   I'm here to save the ice cream, Rocco.

Rocco (*to* **Giuseppe**)   Did you ring her?

Giuseppe *puts the fire-extinguisher down and climbs into the van.*

Bernie   He asked me to come and help. Isn't that great? Giuseppe asked *me*.

Rocco   I don't need any help.

Bernie   You do. You know you do.

The hatch in the van slides open.

Giuseppe (*in van*)   Prendi!

Tubs of ice cream start flying through the hatch. **Rocco** *and* **Bernie** *try to catch them.*

Rocco   Careful, Papa: ice cream is money!

The hatch slides shut again. **Bernie** *and* **Rocco** *start to bag up* *the tubs.*

Bernie   Lino says he won't work today cos it's Good Friday, but he's still let Lulu go out in the van for him.

Rocco   I don't care.

Bernie   She should be working for both of you. Just cos she's Lino's girlfriend doesn't mean she should do everything for him. She was – (*mimes 'split'*) between you.

Rocco   Rocco Raffa walks alone.

Bernie   You don't have to. Giuseppe rung *me*, don't you see? I can be here now. I can help you. There's nothing to stop me.

Rocco   You have to be at home.

Bernie   For what?

Rocco   For the kids. For when they come along.

Bernie   But what if they don't come along?

Rocco   Why wouldn't they come along?

Bernie   It's been a long time, Rocco – and they haven't come along yet.

Rocco   The bedroom's decorated. I can't undecorate it.

Bernie I'm not saying you have to redecorate.

Rocco What about the stars on the ceilin'? What d'yer want me to do with them?

Bernie Don't want you to do anything with them.

Rocco And the swing in the garden? Want me to take that down as well?

Bernie No. Of course not.

Rocco We're doin' what we said we'd do.

Bernie But what we said would happen, hasn't.

Rocco It will.

Bernie I just want to come and work with you. That's all. I know Giuseppe didn't want me to. I know he wanted someone from outside the family, but / I think . . .

Rocco It wasn't Papa, Bernie. It was never him. It was me. (*Beat.*) Wasn't that obvious? It was *me*.

He snatches the bags off **Bernie** *and counts how many tubs they've put in them.* **Bernie** *stares at him.*

Rocco Nine tubs? Should be ten. Where's the tenth tub?

The door of the van slams shut behind **Giuseppe** *as he appears with a tub in one hand and a scoop in the other.*

Rocco Put the lid on it, Papa. We've gotta get it back to the factory.

Giuseppe Have you tasted it?

Rocco I made it.

Giuseppe So you have tasted it?

Rocco 'Course I've tasted it.

Giuseppe Just wanted to check. (*Beat.*) What did you think of it?

Rocco It's . . . fine.

Giuseppe Fine?

Rocco Yeah.

Giuseppe Sure?

Rocco Well, I can't really remember.

Giuseppe Taste it again, Rocco Raffa. Refresh your memory.

Rocco I can't.

Giuseppe You can't?

Rocco Not today.

Giuseppe Why?

Rocco I'm fastin'.

Bernie You don't fast.

Rocco Thought I'd give it a go.

Bernie You had a bacon buttie before you left the house.

Rocco So I fell off the wagon. I'm only human.

Giuseppe You taste it, Bernadette.

Bernie Is it nice? Does it − (*mimes 'taste nice'*)?

Giuseppe You tell me.

Rocco Don't.

Bernie Why?

Rocco You *are* fastin'.

Giuseppe I don't want you to eat it all. Just want you to taste it.

Rocco Still not allowed.

Giuseppe It is.

Rocco Who sez?

Giuseppe I say.

Bernie Just a taste?

Giuseppe Yes.

Rocco No . . .

Giuseppe *passes the scoop to* **Bernie**. **Rocco** *moves towards her. but, as he does so, she tastes the ice cream. There is a pause, then she flinches before recovering herself.*

Giuseppe Well?

Bernie Mmm.

Giuseppe Mmm?

Bernie Mmm. (*Beat.*) Mmm-mmm.

Rocco *smiles and nods.* **Giuseppe** *stares at* **Bernie**. *There is another pause.* **Bernie** *starts to grimace, then pulls a face and wipes her mouth.* **Rocco***'s head slumps.*

Giuseppe This is not gelato!

Rocco It's cost-effective.

Giuseppe This is poison!

Rocco I make it for less and sell it for more.

Giuseppe You don't sell it at all!

Bernie What's in it, Rocco?

Rocco Who cares what's in it?

Giuseppe Vegetable fat? Dried milk?

Rocco It's only ice cream!

Giuseppe For century, we Raffas make squisito gelato, but within few months you are producing *this*?

Rocco People'll buy anythin': they'll eat any ol' shit.

Giuseppe They might buy it once, but won't make same mistake twice. They have always come back for what it *is*. And this *isn't* it.

Rocco   I don't know how to make it!

Giuseppe   You were supposed to learn! (*Beat.*) It's about our name! *Fama*! That's what matters. All *famiglie anziane* are gone – but we remain. We endure. Once, Ancoats was filled with families like ours. But now – just us. And you think that's because of this?

Rocco *shrugs.* **Giuseppe** *throws the tub at him.* **Rocco** *puts the tub into one of the bags.*

Giuseppe   Throw it *all* away.

Bernie   All of it?

Rocco   Think of the money.

Giuseppe   I am! Go back to factory, empty your tanks, and start again.

Rocco   I can't. I've gotta save it. Gotta freeze it.

Giuseppe   You want to freeze. Freeze!

He picks up the fire-extinguisher, turns it on **Rocco** *and sprays and sprays.*

Bernie   Giuseppe!

Giuseppe *drops the fire-extinguisher.*

Giuseppe   Leaves are on trees, Rocco. Days grow longer. Soon children will plead to their parents for gelato. But they won't plead for this. (*Beat.*) We're going to mass. Want van fixed? Do it yourself.

He exits. **Rocco** *is covered with ice crystals.* **Bernie** *pauses for a moment, then follows* **Giuseppe** *– leaving* **Rocco** *still clutching the bags of melted ice cream, and shivering.*

Six

Late May 1990. Garden at rear of Bernie and Rocco's house.

Rocco *sits on a child's swing, with an air-gun in his hand. The rifle is cocked downwards.* **Lino** *enters, carrying a card.*

Lino   Happy birthday, then.

Rocco   Eh?

Lino   Happy birthday.

Lino *smiles and hands* **Rocco** *his birthday card.* **Rocco** *rips open the envelope and checks inside the card for money – but there isn't any.*

Lino   Papa's got you a – a new gun?

Rocco   More than a gun: it's a point one-seven-seven, steel barrelled, spring-pistoned, dovetailed shootin' machine.

Lino (*beat*)   Not real though, is it.

Rocco   What? Am I imaginin' it?

Lino   I mean, it don't fire bullets.

Rocco   Pellets. Could still kill.

Lino   Humans?

Rocco   Animals. Rats 'n' that.

Lino   Have you?

Rocco   What?

Lino   Shot anythin'?

Rocco   Blown the heads of a few flowers.

Lino   What'll Bernie say?

Rocco   Not ours, next door's.

Lino   Oh.

Rocco   Got me a prezzie, then?

Lino   Got you the – the card.

Rocco   What about a prezzie?

Lino   I – I wouldn't know what to get.

Rocco   You coulda put a tenner in, then I coulda got what I want.

Lino   You – you never even get me a card.

Rocco   I always get you sommat to open. (*Beat.*) I mean usually you're inside it / but . . .

Lino   Quiet on the ice-cream front, is it?

Rocco (*beat*)   Who's been sayin' that? I been sellin' plenty, mate.

Lino   Was jus' that Bernie said / that . . .

Rocco   What? What did Bernie say?

Lino   Well . . . nothin' really.

Rocco   Musta been somethin'.

Lino   It wasn't. (*Beat.*) Lulu's been ace. Helpin' me loads.

Rocco   Is that what you call it?

Lino   Bernie'd help you.

Rocco   Rocco . . . walks . . . alone.

Lino   We're shiftin' quite a bit.

Rocco   Why aren't you out now, then?

Lino   She's lookin' after things. Don't know what I'd do without her.

There's a pause, then **Rocco** *points*:

Rocco   Look, Lino: a bird.

Lino   Where?

Rocco   There? Little birdy.

Lino *smiles as he spots the bird.* **Rocco** *snaps the end of the rifle into place.*

Lino   What yer doin'?

Rocco   Target practice.

Lino   Yer can't.

Rocco   It's in my garden. Can do what I like.

Rocco *points the gun and lines it up.*

Lino   Don't.

Rocco *pulls the trigger back, then, just as he is about to fire,* **Lino** *claps his hands together twice. The bird flies away. The gunshot rings out as* **Rocco** *leaps from the swing.*

Rocco   Lino!

Lino   Couldn't jus' let you kill it!

Rocco   What does it matter?!

Lino   What did it do to you?!

Rocco *stares at* **Lino**, *reloads, then points the gun up into the sky and fires. He repeats the process several times without pausing.*

Lino   Stop!

Lino *tries to grab the gun, but* **Rocco** *pushes him away. A handful of feathers fall down from the sky.* **Bernie** *enters carrying a present.* **Rocco** *stops firing.*

Bernie   What're you doing?

Rocco   Showin' him me gun.

Lino   You didn't kill it. You missed.

Rocco *glances at the circle of feathers.*

Rocco   Not by much.

Bernie   Why can't I leave you two alone for a minute? You're not kids any more.

Lino *picks up one of the feathers.* **Bernie** *goes to take the gun off* **Rocco**. *At first, he resists – but when she stares at him, he lets her have it. She cocks the rifle, then hands* **Lino** *the present and motions* *to him to hand it to* **Rocco**. **Lino** *shakes his head, but* **Bernie** *insists.* **Lino** *approaches* **Rocco**.

Rocco   Who's that off?

Lino   Off / Bernie . . .

Bernie   Lino. It's off Lino.

Rocco   It ain't. It's off you.

Bernie   Isn't.

Rocco   You bought it.

Bernie   For him. To give you.

Rocco   Has he paid yer for it?

Bernie   He doesn't need to pay me for it.

Rocco (*to* **Lino**)   Give her the money.

Lino (*to* **Bernie**)   How much was it?

Bernie (*to* **Rocco**)   He does *not* need to pay me.

Rocco   Well, what's the point?

Bernie   Oh, don't make everything into such / a . . .

Rocco   Such a what? Eh? Why can't you jus' keep your mouth shut?

Bernie   What are you – (*mimes 'talking about'*)?

Rocco *grunts and starts to exit.*

Bernie   Where're you going?

Rocco   Out.

Bernie   What about your tea? I'm making you a birthday – (*mimes 'tea'*).

Rocco *turns back, and snatches the present from* **Lino**.

Rocco (*to* **Lino**)   And next time, Rocco won't miss.

He exits again. **Bernie** *stares after him.*

Lino Was only makin' conversation.

Bernie What about?

Lino The business. How I was gettin' on. And how he was.

Bernie Oh.

There is a pause. **Lino** *looks at the feather, then starts to exit.*

Bernie You can't go. I've got a cake. With candles on it.

Lino I can't blow 'em out: it's not my birthday.

Bernie You don't have to blow them out. Just eat the cake.

Lino *stops, and turns back.*

Lino Dunno why he's so moody: I'm not bothered about winnin' anyway. If it wasn't for Lulu helpin' me I'd have no chance.

Bernie She's not helping you Lino – she's doing everything for you. That's not helping. That's very different from helping.

Lino I do stuff.

Bernie Not enough. Do more. Do your bit. Do as much as you can.

Lino Why should I?

Bernie Cos you've got to win!

Pause.

Lino Bernie?

Bernie I want *you* to win, Lino.

She takes the feather from **Lino** *and hands him the gun.*

Bernie I want to work. I want to – (*mimes 'help'*). That might seem – (*mimes 'crazy'*) to everyone, but it's – (*mimes 'true'*).

Lino But what can I do about that?

Bernie Rocco won't let me work for him. Ever. But you would. I could work for you.

Lino *takes the pellets from the gun. He holds them in his open palm, then drops the gun.*

Lino I don't like fightin'.

Bernie It's not about fightin'. It's about tryin'. Just do your best. And don't do it for me: do it for you.

Lino For me?

Bernie Think you'd enjoy workin' for Rocco?

Lino I've been workin' for him for years.

Bernie No – you've been working *with* him. You've been working *for* Giuseppe.

Lino *thinks for a moment, then sits down on the swing.*

Bernie I used to believe in Rocco. Used to. But now? I want to, I try to, but every time I've been out, and I get back home, another few bricks have gone from my garden wall. Thought I was imagining it at first, but . . . it used to be – (*mimes 'high'*) and now it's – (*mimes 'low'*). How can you believe in someone who does that and thinks I won't even notice? Thinks I walk around with my eyes – (*mimes 'closed'*).

Lino I believe in you, Bernie. And if I won, I really would want you to work with me.

Bernie *starts to push the swing, its rusty chain squeaking as it moves.*

Lino I'd want you. And I'd want Lulu. Cos I believe in her, too.

Bernie It's still early days, Lino. You hardly know her.

Lino Know what I need to know. I mean, I know I've not had *many* girlfriends, / but . . .

Bernie Many?

Lino OK – *any* – but I – I still know what I feel . . . y'know?

Bernie *nods.*

Lino   Told her that I love her.

Bernie   And what did she say?

Lino   Said she'd break my heart.

Bernie   Oh.

Lino   But she won't.

Bernie   How d'you know?

Lino   Cos I know . . . what I feel . . . I know . . . that I *do* love her. And I *do* believe in her.

Bernie *stops pushing the swing.*

Bernie   So what're you gonna do?

Lino   I'll do my best. For me. For you. And for Lulu.

I really will try.

Bernie *looks down at the feather in her hand as* **Lino***'s swinging gets slower and slower — till all that's left is the squeak of the chain.*

Seven

Production area of Raffa's ice-cream factory. Continuous.

On the wall is a control panel with a jumble of wires jutting out precariously from behind it. Further along are a few hooks on which hang white jackets and overalls, blue boots and hair-nets. There is the hum of machinery as the pasteurisation tank heats the ice cream, the holding tank cools it and the mixing machine adds different flavours. **Lulu** *wears a white jacket, blue hair net and blue boots. She holds a tub beneath the nozzle of the mixing machine.* **Rocco** *enters and watches her. She moves the tub round so that the ice cream continues to spread evenly until it runs out.*

Rocco   So you're even makin' the ice cream for him now, are yer?

Lulu   Thought you were at the birthday party.

Rocco   Had other plans.

Lulu   It's your birthday.

Rocco   You've not put enough stuff in – that's why it's run out.

Lulu   I put the perfect amount in: this is all I wanted to make.

Lulu *dips a tasting-stick into the ice cream and licks it.*

Rocco   Got sommat for you 'ere. Sommat you might want.

He takes a stone from his inside pocket and holds it up to the light.

Lulu   What is it?

Rocco   An actual piece of the Berlin Wall.

Lulu   Piss off.

Rocco   This is history is this. Proper history.

Lulu   How did you get it?

Rocco   Did a deal, di'n' I. Here: have a hold.

Lulu *puts her tub on top of the tank and takes the stone from* **Rocco**.

Lulu   Weird, innit? Just looks dead normal. Like a bit o' brick from any old wall.

Rocco *grabs it back from her.*

Rocco   What do you know? Have you ever been to Berlin?

Lulu   No.

Rocco   Well then.

Lulu   Wasn't bein' funny, was jus' sayin'.

Rocco   Be worth a shedload o' money, this.

Lulu   Yer think?

Rocco   I know. (*Beat.*) Yer can have it if you want.

Lulu Can I? Thanks.

She takes the stone from him.

Rocco I'll cut you a deal: as it's you . . . only a tenner.

Lulu You want me to pay for it?

Rocco It'd be an investment.

Lulu Piss off.

She throws the stone back to **Rocco**. *He puts it in his pocket angrily.*

Rocco You wanna watch what yer say: he might be your boyfriend, but he's no more your boss than me. You were split between us. You're half-mine.

Lulu (*beat*) Which half do you want?

She takes her hairnet off and shakes her hair out.

Rocco You've got to keep that on in 'ere.

Lulu I won't tell anyone if you don't.

She picks up the tub again and samples some more of her ice cream.

Rocco Let me have some of that, then.

Lulu No.

Rocco I want some.

Lulu Well, you can't have any.

Rocco I'm not gonna pay for ice cream in my own factory.

Lulu Good, cos it aint for sale.

Rocco To me?

Lulu To anyone. I'm jus' practisin'. Messin' around. Tryin' out different flavours. Lino said I could.

Rocco And what's that? Vanilla?

Lulu Oh, it might look like vanilla. But it's much more than that. Believe me.

Rocco   Let me taste it then.

Lulu   Can I taste yours?

Rocco   No.

Lulu   See.

Rocco   But / it's . . .

Lulu   But nothin'.

She tastes some more of her own ice cream.

Rocco (*beat*)   OK then.

Lulu   OK what?

Rocco   OK.

*He marches over to one of the tanks, pulls the lid back, dunks the dipstick in, and offers it to **Lulu**. She laughs, then tastes it. Another drip drops down from the roof. There is a pause, then **Lulu** pulls a face.*

Rocco   Piss off! So Lino's shown you how to make it? So you think you're sommat? Piss right off. You know nothin'!

Lulu   Touchy, / aren't yer . . .

Rocco   Well, / I mean . . .

Lulu   It don't taste nice. Simple as.

Rocco   Gimme some o' yours, then.

Lulu   Nah.

Rocco   But you've had some of mine.

Lulu   So?

Rocco   You said / that . . .

Lulu   No, I didn't.

She has some more of her own ice cream.

Rocco   You're havin' some!

Lulu (*laughs*)   I've gotta get rid o' the taste o' yours!

Rocco *throws the dipstick to the floor. Another drip falls.*

Rocco   You can do his accounts, and you can do his orderin'. You can make it, and you can sell it. But you won't win. You can't beat Rocco Raffa. (*Beat.*) You backed the wrong horse.

Lulu   I didn't back any horse.

Rocco (*beat*)   Rain leaks through the roof. And gas from the pasteurisation tank. Papa built this place. And it's fallin' apart.

Lulu   I'n't that dangerous? The gas. Don't yer need an extractor thing? Or air-conditionin'?

Rocco *points up near the roof and nods.*

Rocco   Papa built that 'n' all. But no one's switched it on in years. Prob'ly blow up.

Lulu   So why don't yer get it fixed? Get it *all* fixed.

Rocco   Yer can't keep fixin' things for ever. It's easier to knock 'em down and start again. (*Beat.*) And besides, I keep me ciggies up there.

Lulu   Up there?

Rocco   What Bernie don't know won't hurt her.

Lulu   Are you afraid to do all the things you want to, Rocco?

Rocco   Rocco's not afraid of anythin'.

The drips start to drop between them at increasingly regular intervals.
Lulu *has some more of her ice cream.*

Lulu   When did yer last cry?

Rocco   Never.

Lulu   Bet yer did, *ever*. When you was a kid.

Rocco   Not tellin' yer.

Lulu If you do, you can taste my ice cream.

Rocco You said that before.

Lulu I didn't!

Pause.

I never even cried when me dad left – but that was only cos I didn't know he wasn't ever comin' back. If I had've known, I guess I would.

She scoops up some more of her ice cream and passes the scoop to **Rocco**. *He goes to taste it, but she puts her hand on his wrist and stops him. Pause.*

Rocco Jus' before Lino was born, Mamma brought me 'ere to see Papa. And I climbed up onto the holdin' tank to try and reach the ice cream. Try and taste it.

Lulu And did yer?

Rocco I fell in.

Lulu *laughs.*

Rocco Wasn't funny. Coulda drowned. (*Beat.*) Mamma saved me. Fished me out and cleaned me up. I tried to hug her, but couldn't get my hands around the bump. (*Beat.*) Papa jus' screamed at me for ruinin' all the ice cream.

Lulu And you cried?

Rocco (*nods*) Always felt older than I was, and bigger than I was, but *then* – covered head-to foot in ice cream – I felt little and weak and that. Felt like I was. And didn't ever wanna feel that way again.

Lulu But what about when your mam died – you must o' cried then?

Rocco I was your age.

Lulu You're still allowed to cry.

Rocco (*beat*) Well, I didn't, alright?

Lulu *lets go of* **Rocco***'s wrist. He tastes some of the ice cream from the scoop. There is a pause, then he tastes some more. There is another pause, then he takes the whole tub from* **Lulu***. She laughs.*

Rocco   What's in this?

Lulu   Secret.

Rocco   We've gotta sell it.

Lulu   We?

Rocco   This would sell.

Lulu   Ain't for sale. I said. Jus' for me.

Rocco *(beat)*   With him, everythin'll be a struggle. With me, whatever you want is yours.

Lulu   Rocco . . .

Rocco   Soon be summer. And that's when the competition really begins. Stay with him and you might win. Come with me, and you can't lose. *(Beat.)* Play with fire, Lulu. Play with fire.

The drips from the roof drop faster and faster. **Lulu** *steps closer to* **Rocco** *– directly beneath the leak – then tilts her head back, so the rainwater falls onto her face.* **Rocco** *lunges at her, kissing her.* **Lulu** *pulls away.*

Lulu   What yer doin'?

Rocco   What d'yer mean?

Lulu   I'm your brother's girlfriend!

Rocco   So?

Lulu   You're married!

Rocco   So what?

Lulu   So you can't!

Rocco   I want you.

Lulu   You can't have me.

Rocco   You want me.

Lulu   We were talkin' about business. A workin' relationship.

Rocco   No we weren't. (*Beat.*) Were we?

Lulu   Was about the ice cream. Just about the ice cream.

Rocco *looks at* **Lulu** *hopelessly as she steps back from the rain. He throws her tub back to her, then turns angrily to the roof.*

Rocco   When will the fuckin' rain stop? It's even followin' me indoors now!

As **Rocco**'s *shout reverberates, the flap of wings is heard from up above.* **Rocco** *turns away from* **Lulu** *and starts to walk off. She lifts the tub and presses her face into it so that it's covered in ice cream.*

Lulu   I've *always* played with fire, Rocco. And when I play, I *do* play to win.

Rocco *turns back, then walks tentatively towards her. He stretches his arm out, and runs his finger down her cheek – leaving streaks of flesh beneath the ice cream.*

Lulu   If yer liked my ice cream that much, I don't see why you shouldn't have some more.

Rocco   What's in it?

Lulu   Wanna know me secrets? Come 'ere then.

Lulu *puts her mouth next to* **Rocco**'s *ear and whispers something to him – then kisses him softly and steps away.* **Rocco** *licks the ice cream round his lips.*

Lulu   How do I taste now?

Rocco   You taste good.

He starts to lick the ice cream from off her face, her forehead, her cheeks, her nose, then back down to her lips.

Eight

*Early June 1990. Raffa's ice cream van parked on the recreation
ground off Rochdale Road, Manchester.*

The ventilation hatch in the roof of the van opens and **Lino***'s hands
appear. He pulls himself up and through it – then sits on the roof with
his feet dangling down inside the van.* **Lulu** *is visible through the
windows.*

Lulu (*in van*) What yer doin'?

Lino Come up.

Lulu (*in van*) You won't sell any ice cream round 'ere.

Lino Should see the view.

Lulu (*in van*) Don't wanna see the view.

Lino Can see the whole o' Manchester.

Lulu (*in van*) Wonderful.

Lino Really is.

Lulu (*in van*) I came to give you a hand, not park up on
the rec and sit on the roof.

Lino *swings his legs up onto the roof and looks down into the van
through the hatch.*

Lino Come on, Lulu.

Lulu (*in van*) No.

Lino It's important.

Lulu (*in van*) It's not important.

She clambers up, sticks her head through the hatch and looks at **Lino** *–
who sits cross-legged on the roof.*

Lulu Sellin' ice cream's important!

Lino I'm tryin'.

Lulu Are yer?

Lino I'm *learnin'*.

Lulu Not quick enough.

Lino Takes a while – gettin' the hang o' things – but I think I'm gettin' there.

Lulu I don't.

Pause.

Lino Feel like I'm losin'.

Lulu You are. Or you're gonna. (*Beat.*) We were kiddin' ourselves thinkin' shiftin' a few cornets in spring counted for anythin'.

Lino Didn't mean the competition. Meant you.

Lulu Eh?

Lino Feel like I'm losin' *you*.

Lulu It's not about me. It's about the ice cream.

Lulu *lifts her arms through the hatch and bangs her elbows down onto the roof.*

Lulu It's nearly summer, Lino. And you won't be able to compete with Rocco.

Lino We *are* competin' with him.

Lulu But we know he's gonna win. (*Beat.*) So give up. Give in.

Lino *shifts to a crouching position.*

Lino That's all I've – all I've ever done. And I'm not doin' it any more. The people of Manchester deserve better.

Lulu The people of Manchester?

Lino I didn't wanna fight, Lulu. So I let you fight for me. But now I am. And I know that it matters. That it means sommat. And I'm not jus' fightin' for me, or Bernie, / or . . .

Lulu Bernie?

Lino   Or you. I'm fightin' for everyone. The ice cream people want is the one they've always had. And I'm the only person who can give it to 'em.

Lulu   Yer can't, though!

Lino   I can!

Lulu   No!

She shakes her head then lowers herself back into the van, but, just as her gloved hands are about to disappear, **Lino** *grabs them.*

Lulu (*in van*)   Lino!

Lino *stands slowly, lifting* **Lulu** *up through the hatch. She tries to escape his grip, but he doesn't let go till he's pulled her through and she's sitting on the roof, with only her legs dangling back into the van.*

Lulu (*in van*)   Let go!

Lino   You've gotta believe in me, Lulu.

Lulu   Well, I don't. And you shouldn't believe in me.

Lino   But I do.

Lulu   Stop then.

Lino   I can't.

Lulu   I'm not Lois Lane, Lino: I'm kryptonite!

A car drives past. She glances over in the direction of the sound.

Did you see them lookin'? Must think you're crazy.

Lino   Stand up.

Lulu   I'm not standin' up. It aint safe.

Lino   You wanted me to jump the canal in the pitch black, but you're too scared to stand on the roof of a van?

Lulu   I'm not scared, it's jus' . . .

Lino *offers his hand to* **Lulu**. *This time she takes it voluntarily. He helps her to stand. She's a little unsteady at first, but* **Lino** *continues to hold her hand as they look out.*

Lino Know it don't always look much close up, but –
from *here*, well – could be a London or a Paris or / a . . .

Lulu Have you ever been to London or Paris?

Lino Well, no, but I mean – might not be a place for the
high and mighty – for poets or politicians, but . . . people . . .
yeah, a place for the people.

Lulu Dead windy, innit.

Lino Lulu, *look*.

Lulu I am lookin'.

Lino And?

Lulu Looks alright, yeah.

Lino Mamma used to bring me up here. I'd lean into the
wind. And let it hold me up. Felt like I was flyin'.

Lulu Gonna piss it down in a minute.

Lino Haven't *you* got anywhere? A special place or sommat?

Pause.

Lulu Me dad used to take me round Roman remains.
Sounds a bit rubbish that, don't it . . . but I used to like it.

Lino Doesn't sound rubbish at all.

Lulu Well, you wouldn't think so – but everyone else would.
I mean, you're sort o' like him. A bit naff. In a sweet way.

Lino Naff?

Lulu He'd point and show me where things were. And
there wasn't anythin' to see most o' the time. Just grooves in
a hill. But he'd tell me what it would've looked like . . .
what people would've been doin' and that. And I felt like I
could see it. Felt like I was there.

Suddenly, **Lino** *drops onto one knee. The roof of the van shakes and*
Lulu *loses her balance for a second.* **Lino** *steadies her.*

Lino   Saved your life. (*Beat.*) I won't lose you, Lulu. Now that I've got you, I'm not gonna let go. So . . . marry me, then.

Lino *takes a small box from his pocket and flips it open to reveal: a scuffed, slightly bent engagement ring with a very small diamond.* **Lulu** *trembles.*

Lino   Was Mamma's. I know the diamond's only little, but look at it close . . . shaped like a cornet. Papa did that.

Lulu   It's lovely.

Lino   So what d'yer think?

Lulu *turns away from him and looks out across the city.*

Lulu   Always wanted somebody to do this for me. Somethin' jus' like this.

Lino   Well, I have – I've done it.

Lulu   Why? Why have yer? Yer can't / jus' . . .

Lino   I know I – I can be a bit hopeless and that. That there's loads o' people better than me. Who're brighter than me. And braver than me. But I won't ever let yer down.

Lulu   Oh, Lino.

Lino   Or rather, I will – I mean, me bein' me, I'm bound to. Might even do it often. But I will never ever mean to. Will never ever plan to. Never ever let yer down on purpose.

Lulu   But what if I let *you* down?

Lino   You won't.

Lulu   What if I have?

Lino   I forgive yer.

Lulu   Not as simple as that: you don't know what I've done. Coulda done anythin'. I said I'd break your heart – maybe I have. (*Beat.*) Yer can't jus' forgive someone like that.

Lino   I have done. (*Beat.*) Jus' think you're an angel.

Lulu   Must be a sign o' the times then − if even the Angels are ordinary now.

Lino   Nah, it's not about havin' wings and that. It's . . . I mean . . . I've never met anyone like you.

Lulu   Believe me, I am nothin'.

Lino   Ain't about what you *are* − or what anythin' *is* − it's about what you *can be*. And you can be bloody extraordinary.

Lulu   You're wrong.

Lino   I'm not. I've seen it. I can see it.

Lulu *turns her back to him and holds her hands up hopelessly.*

Lulu   My gloves.

Lino   What about 'em?

Lulu   I won't take 'em off.

Lino   So?

Lulu   So even if I wore a ring, no one'd see it. No one'd know.

Lino   I'd know. (*Beat.*) I want yer.

Lulu   Yer don't.

Lino   I do.

Lulu   Yer do?

Lino   I *do*. (*Beat.*) So . . . do you?

Lulu *looks down at* **Lino** *holding the ring − then at her gloved hands.*

Nine

Continuous. Dining room of Giuseppe's house.

Giuseppe *sits on his chair.* **Bernie** *kneels in front of him, painting his face in red, white and green stripes.*

Bernie   Eyes.

Giuseppe   What?

Bernie   Close your eyes.

Giuseppe   But / –

Bernie   Close them.

Giuseppe *closes his eyes.*

Giuseppe   How can you say that?

Bernie   What?

Giuseppe   That you don't want Rocco to win.

Bernie   I don't.

Giuseppe   Bernadette!

Bernie   But I *really* don't want him to lose.

Giuseppe   Those that can't win, *must* lose.

Bernie   I'm worried about him.

Giuseppe   Don't worry about him – worry about biz.

Bernie   He's working so hard.

Giuseppe   Needs to work harder.

Bernie   He can't.

Giuseppe   He's got to.

Bernie   He comes home late – sleeps in the spare room so he won't wake me up – then first thing in the morning, he's out again. (*Beat.*) I looked in on him the other night, and he was wide awake. Just lying there. Staring at the stars on the ceiling.

Giuseppe All that work, and still no sales.

Bernie Cos he just can't make ice cream like you and Lino can. (*Beat.*) He can't learn how to make it, but Lino *is* learning how to sell it.

Giuseppe Everything will change when schools break up. That six weeks will decide everything.

Bernie I know you just want the one who sells the most to win, / but . . .

Giuseppe I want Rocco to win! Merlino's Mammi Bambino without Mamma. Not sort of man you work for, but sort of man who works for you.

Bernie Then end the competition. Stop it now. And share the business.

Giuseppe This is not co-operative. We're in Manchester, not Rochdale. Competition ends only with result. Imagine those two: wars without winners go on an' on, and I can't keep peace forever.

Bernie No, but I can.

Giuseppe You're not always there.

Bernie I could be. I want to work, and I could work between them. You want us all to learn? We could all learn (*mimes 'together'*).

Giuseppe People don't learn together. They learn alone.

Bernie (*beat*) Can open your eyes now.

Giuseppe *opens his eyes.*

Giuseppe Biz is dying, Bernadette.

Bernie Dying?

Giuseppe We make squisito gelato. And people want it, because they know it's best. It's Raffa's. And they think, 'As soon as rain stops, we'll come, we'll buy.' But it never stops in this city of rain. What did we do wrong to end up ice-cream men here? It always falls. And we're dying with every drop.

Bernie   Didn't know.

Giuseppe   I couldn't keep it going any longer. Much more and we'll go to wall.

Bernie   What can we do?

Giuseppe   I need my boy to take it on. Need my boy to be man.

Bernie   You want Rocco?

Giuseppe   I want leader. (*Beat.*)

Bernie   Lips. Close mouth.

Giuseppe *closes his mouth again and* **Bernie** *begins to apply paint around it. There is a pause, then she speaks:*

Bernie   I want a role, Giuseppe. In the business. I want to do something.

Giuseppe *goes to reply, but:*

Bernie   Lips! (*Beat.*) I stay at home to look after my children. And I don't have any children.

Giuseppe *goes to speak again, but:*

Bernie   *Lips!* (*Beat.*) It isn't going to happen. Can't happen. And maybe we're better off without screaming kids all around us. I don't know. (*Beat.*) Just know that if I don't do something, I'll go mad. I *need* to do something. (*Beat.*) Speak then.

Giuseppe   All my life, I've been so busy making gelato and selling gelato that I've never had chance to see people enjoy it. So now I want to sit back and count the / people . . .

Bernie   Money?

Giuseppe   *People.* In queues at my vans. Is that so wrong?

Bernie   And is it so wrong for me to want to help?

Giuseppe (*beat*)   I won't share biz, Bernadette, but I *will* find something for you to do. And when opportunity arises, you *can* do it.

Lino *and* **Lulu** *enter, holding hands*

Bernie   Just in time.

Lino   For what?

Giuseppe   *For what?!*

Bernie   The – (*mimes 'football'.*)

Bernie *motions towards* **Giuseppe**'s *finished face.*

Lino   Oh. Right.

Giuseppe   *Oh. Right.*

Lulu   We've got news.

Giuseppe   Now is not time for news. Now is time for calcio.

Lino   It's important news.

Giuseppe   This is Mondiali – doesn't get more important than that.

Rocco *enters. He holds an ice cream in one hand and a black leather briefcase in the other. The ice cream has started to melt and run down his hand.*

Rocco   You need to taste this, Papa.

Lulu (*to* **Rocco**)   Hiya.

Bernie   Game kicks off in a min.

Rocco   England don't play / until . . .

Giuseppe   Italia! Italia!

Lino   We – we said we've got news.

Rocco (*to* **Giuseppe**)   You *have* to taste it.

Bernie   Let's just watch the – (*mimes 'football' again*).

Giuseppe (*to* **Rocco**)   You're going to poison me again?

Rocco Taste.

Bernie What's in it for Rocco?

Rocco Yer think I can't make real ice cream. Magical ice cream. Or – you think I can make the ice cream, but not the magic. Well, Rocco can. Rocco has. Angel ice cream. Angelato. Taste it. Taste the magic.

Lino Is anybody listenin' to me?

Bernie The game, Giuseppe, it's – (*mimes 'kicking off'*).

Giuseppe *claps his hands together twice. There is silence.*

Giuseppe Sit.

Reluctantly, **Bernie** *sits down at one side of the table.* **Lulu** *sits at the other.* **Giuseppe** *takes a handkerchief from his pocket and grasps* **Rocco***'s ice cream with it. He lifts the cone up in the air, checks the ice cream against the light, then looks at* **Rocco** *and* **Lino***. They sit down too:* **Rocco** *next to* **Bernie***;* **Lino** *next to* **Lulu***.*
Giuseppe *inches the ice cream closer and closer to his mouth, then licks it. Puccini's 'Nessun Dorma', sung by Pavarotti, starts to play in.* **Giuseppe** *licks it twice more. He looks deadly serious – as if something immense is happening – then the sides of his pursed lips turn up into a hardly discernable smile. The smile becomes bigger and bigger till it covers his face.* **Rocco** *starts to smile too. 'Nessun Dorma' becomes louder as* **Giuseppe** *stands and holds the ice cream aloft.*

Lino We're – we're getting' married.

Bernie Married?

Giuseppe (*beat*) Magico.

Bernie *looks at* **Lino***.* **Lino** *looks at* **Lulu***.* **Lulu** *looks at* **Rocco***.* **Rocco** *looks at* **Giuseppe** *– and* **Giuseppe** *looks at the ice cream.*

Interval.

Act Two

One

Early September 1990. Storage area of Raffa's ice-cream factory.

Large wooden boxes and smaller cardboard ones are scattered around the floor. **Lino** *picks up cardboard box after cardboard box and places them in a line.* **Giuseppe** *speaks as he watches him.*

Giuseppe   Everybody's screaming for ice cream!

Lino   I've been doin' OK.

Giuseppe   You've done well, Merlino. But have you seen queues at Rocco's van?

Lino   Heard about 'em.

Giuseppe   We have invented Angelato. Kids of Manchester are lapping it up. And even though holidays are over, now every season can be summer.

Lino *kicks the row of boxes into place.*

Giuseppe   Watch wafers!

Lino *glares at* **Giuseppe**, *then starts to pile another row of boxes onto the first one.* **Giuseppe** *is standing on the other side of it from* **Lino**.

Lino   Are yer gonna help me?

Giuseppe   I'm retired.

Lino   You're here.

Giuseppe   I'm here, / but . . .

Lino   But not to help?

Giuseppe   Not to lift boxes, / or . . .

Lino   Just to watch?

Giuseppe   I built this place! Put this roof over your head.

Lino   It leaks.

Giuseppe   Then fix it! Days of me doing things for you have gone. I'm retired. And can do whatever I want. And if I want to watch, I'll watch.

Lino *bangs the boxes down hard again as he starts on a third row.*

Giuseppe   Wafers!

Pause.

Lino   I – I really do need you to help me, Papa.

Giuseppe   I told you / I'm . . .

Lino   Not with the boxes.

Giuseppe   Then with what?

Lino   Bernie convinced me that if I really tried and gave it my best shot, I could win. But I have. And I can't. It's not enough. (*Beat.*) So why wait another two months till Mamma's birthday?

Giuseppe   There is no rush.

Lino   I can take bein' beaten, Papa, but I can't take bein' beaten every single day.

Giuseppe   You are doing well. And Rocco's doing great. Biz is thriving.

Lino   But Rocco's gonna win. Lulu's been sayin' it for ages. And even Bernie says it now.

Giuseppe   Only things that I say matter.

Lino   I want you to tell him that the business is his – that he can have it now – as long as he doesn't sack me.

Giuseppe   Rocco wouldn't sack you.

Lino   Don't let him take my ice cream away.

Giuseppe   Man cannot live by gelato alone, Merlino.

Lino   It's all I know.

Giuseppe   You could learn something else.

Lino   He's gonna sack me, and he's gonna sack Lulu. And you're gonna let him?

Giuseppe   He *won't* sack you.

Lino   When he takes over, the first thing / he'll do . . .

Giuseppe   *If* he takes over, / then . . .

Lino   If?

Giuseppe   There are few certainties in life.

Lino   You honestly think I've still got a chance?

Giuseppe *(laughs)*   You? No!

Lino   Then who?

Giuseppe   It's not as / simple as . . .

Lino   You?

Giuseppe *(laughs)*   Me? No-no-no.

Lino   Then why the 'if'?

Giuseppe   Anything might happen.

Lino   *What* might happen?

Giuseppe   Biz might be . . . sold.

Lino *stops piling the boxes and peers over the cardboard wall that has built up between himself and* **Giuseppe**.

Lino   Sold?

Giuseppe   Sold.

Lino   You can't do that.

Giuseppe   There's nothing I can't do.

Lino   But Bernie reckoned you said the business was worthless anyway.

Giuseppe   Well, Bernie's boccalone! She shouldn't've said, should she? *(Beat.)* And worthless? I did not say worthless. Cos it wasn't. Or isn't. Not now.

Lino   What about all the money we owe?

Giuseppe   On my way here, man came up to me in street – after tasting Angelato, he'd wept with wonder at beauty of sky. And phoned his mother to tell her about it.

Lino   Oh, come on . .

Giuseppe   Is truth! Angelato is sensation. We won't owe anything any more. People will owe us.

Lino   So?

Giuseppe   No.

Lino   Tell me what's goin' on!

Pause.

Giuseppe   Don't breathe word to Rocco.

Lino   Just tell me.

Giuseppe   Don't.

Lino   I won't.

Giuseppe   Who's to say our success hasn't made *ragazzi grande* sit up and take notice? Hasn't made them want piece of action? Want what we've got?

Lino   You know somethin'?

Giuseppe   Say there'd been offer. For whole biz.

Lino   For someone else to take over?

Giuseppe   Lot of money, Merlino.

Lino   Has there been?

Giuseppe   Don't tell me you wouldn't take it. Don't tell me I can't.

Lino   There has, hasn't there?

Giuseppe   But not enough. Oh no. We've got licence to print money here. So we wait. And soon, they'll offer even more.

Lino   You can't sell!

Giuseppe   Watch me.

Lino   What about Rocco?

Giuseppe (*shrugs*)   What about Rocco?

Lino   And me. And Lulu. And Bernie. What about us?

Giuseppe   Gelato didn't give me life. It took one away. Now we can free ourselves from it. (*Beat.*) You'll be able to go out into world and do whatever you want.

Lino   Rocco wants the business. He's always wanted the business.

Giuseppe   He'll get over it.

Lino   That's why you won't tell him – that's why you don't want him to know.

Giuseppe   I don't want him to know cos he wouldn't understand. Not right now. (*Beat.*) But he will one day.

Pause.

Lino   I never used to want it at all. But now – d'you know what? – I really do. (*Beat.*) Why wait till I finally want somethin', before tellin' me I can't have it?

Giuseppe   You'll both be OK.

Lino   But what if we're not?

Giuseppe   I thought that it was time for my family to look after me, but I was wrong. Family can't. Only money can.

Lino   You have to change your mind.

Giuseppe   The ice-cream man's not for turning.

Lino *starts hurriedly to pile box after box on top of the wall.*

Giuseppe   Merlino?

The wall gets higher and higher. When **Lino** *has disappeared completely from* **Giuseppe**'s *view, he stops. On one side of the wall,*

Lino *puts his head in his hands and wipes his eyes – whilst on the other,* **Giuseppe** *shouts:*

Giuseppe Merlino!

He marches round the wall, but as he does so **Lino** *goes round the other way – so they are both still on opposite sides.* **Lino** *and* **Giuseppe** *glare at the boxes between them. There is a pause, then* **Lino** *throws himself into the wall, kicking out and shoulder-barging the boxes simultaneously, making them topple and scatter.* **Giuseppe** *narrowly avoids them as he comes face to face with* **Lino**.

Giuseppe You've broken them all!

Lino You can't just turn around / and . . .

Giuseppe I'm going to take this out of your wages.

Lino And ignore your responsibilities!

Giuseppe When will you grow up? It's about time you saw what real world is all about.

Lino I have seen it. Or I'm startin' to. It's you who can't. Not me.

Giuseppe *claps his hands together twice, but* **Lino** *continues.*

Lino You think if you close your eyes to something it doesn't happen . . .

Giuseppe *claps his hands together twice again, but still* **Lino** *continues.*

Lino But whilst you were in your van – rather than by Mamma's bed – she got sicker, not better . . .

Giuseppe *slaps* **Lino** *across the face.* **Lino** *stops. There is a pause, then he steps towards* **Giuseppe** *and holds out his hands to him, but* **Giuseppe** *leans over, rips open one of the boxes, and pulls out a handful of broken wafers.*

Giuseppe It's great offer. Money is unbelievable. And we'll get more. More we sell – more we'll sell for.

Lino *exits.* **Giuseppe** *rubs his finger and thumb together, shards of wafer falling from his hand.*

Two

Late September 1990. Castlefield Roman remains, Manchester.

An ice-cream jingle version of 'Step On' by Happy Mondays plays for a few seconds, before coming to an abrupt halt along with the engine. **Lulu** *sits on the remains of a wall.* **Rocco** *enters, carrying his briefcase in one hand and two cornets in the other.*

Rocco   Just had a group o' kids chasin' me all down Deansgate. Chasin' the van. How cool's that?

Lulu   You're not the Pied Piper, Rocco.

Rocco   The Pied Piper of Manchester. I like that.

Lulu   I don't. (*Beat.*) And when we're meetin', don't play the music. Not much of a secret now, is it?

Rocco   Get this down you.

Rocco *puts his briefcase down, then passes one of the cornets to* **Lulu**. *He sits down next to her and they both start to devour their ice creams.*

Lulu   Weird 'ere, innit?

Rocco   You picked it, not me.

Lulu   Before everythin' else, though – before there was a Manchester – there was this. Just this. (*Beat.*) Musta built it well.

Rocco   Who?

Lulu   The Romans.

Rocco   Italians, see. Yer can't go wrong.

Lulu   Don't reckon anythin' built now'll last this long.

Rocco   Who cares what lasts?

Lulu   You.

Rocco   Rocco Raffa says 'knock everythin' down!'

Lulu   You're still with her.

Rocco Eh?

Lulu Bernie.

Rocco Not for long.

Lulu No?

Rocco No.

He forces his cornet into his mouth, then leans over to **Lulu** *and starts to kiss her neck. A train thunders across the viaduct above them.* **Lulu** *pulls away from* **Rocco**, *and jumps up.*

Lulu When then?

Rocco When what?

Lulu Are you gonna leave her?

Rocco Could leave anytime.

Lulu Could you?

Rocco All I ever wanted from her was a son. A boy o' me own. A Raffa. An heir. (*Beat.*) And she can't even give me that.

Lulu Maybe . . .

Rocco What?

Lulu We could have one. One day.

There is a pause. She picks up a loose Roman stone and rolls it over in her glove.

Rocco She only lived round the corner when we was kids. Used to follow me everywhere. Was always tellin' her to stop. But she wouldn't. Couldn't.

Lulu And eventually you stopped tellin'?

Rocco Somethin' like that, yeah.

Lulu Demolish her, Rocco.

Rocco I will.

Lulu When yer do . . .

Rocco   Yeah?

Lulu   Yer think she'll cry?

Rocco   Her eyes out.

He stands up and goes to kiss **Lulu** *again. As he does so, another train thunders across the viaduct.* **Lulu** *pulls away once more and sits down.* **Rocco** *huffs agitatedly.*

Lulu   It'll be me and you then, won't it? Raffa's'll be all ours.

Rocco   It'll be mine. But you'll help. You'll be there. Obviously.

Lulu   More than there. Not just a . . . employee. More than that. Be us. Be ours. (*Beat.*) Not straight away – till it's all died down and everybody's forgot I was ever engaged to Lino 'n' that. Not till then. But then? Yeah. Yeah. Yeah?

Rocco (*beat*)   Yeah.

Lulu   Everythin'll work out. I know it will. (*Beat. Smiles.*) Wouldn't wanna make an enemy o' me, would yer?

Rocco   What's that s'posed to mean?

Lulu (*smiles*) Nothin'. Just a joke.

Rocco   You threatenin' me?

Lulu (*smiles*) No.

Rocco   Don't threaten me.

Lulu (*smiles*)   I'm not.

Rocco   Cos you wouldn't ever say anythin'. You wouldn't ever tell anybody anythin'. I know you wouldn't.

Lulu (*smiles*) You're right: I wouldn't.

Rocco (*smiles*)   Good. That's good.

Lulu (*laughs*)   If I did, what would yer do?

Rocco (*laughs*)   If you did, I'd break your legs.

Lulu (*laughs*)   Are you threatenin' me?

Rocco (*laughs*)   No.

Lulu (*laughs*)   You better not be.

Rocco (*laughs*)   I'm jokin'. I'm jokin' 'n' all. It's a joke.

Lulu (*laughs*)   It's not funny.

Rocco (*laughs*)   You're laughin'.

Lulu (*smiles*)   But I don't find it funny.

Rocco (*smiles*)   Then it's an unfunny joke.

Lulu (*smiles*)   Is it?

Rocco (*smiles*)   What I'm sayin' is – I wouldn't threaten you. I've no need to, have I? Cos we're talkin' about sommat you'd never do. Aren't we?

Lulu (*smiles*)   Yeah.

Rocco (*smiles*)   Yeah.

Lulu *tosses the Roman stone to* **Rocco**. *He repeatedly throws it up in the air and catches it.*

Lulu   When d'you want me to go and see our Joe next?

Rocco   I don't.

Lulu   Why?

Rocco   What is goin' on with his face at all?

Lulu   He had an accident. When he was a kid.

Rocco   Well it *freaks* me out. (*Beat.*) I won't be needin' his help any more.

Lulu   Cos of his face?

Rocco   No.

Lulu   Are you stoppin' then? Is that why?

Rocco   Eh?

Lulu   Puttin' it in the ice cream?

Rocco   No.

Lulu   Why then?

Rocco   We've got enough up in the air-conditionin' unit for now.

Lulu   And when that's gone?

Rocco   I don't need to use your brother. Can use anybody.

Pause.

Lulu   Angelato was never meant to be sold, Rocco. (*Beat.*) I thought you jus' wanted to show Giuseppe you could make ice cream that tasted great.

Rocco   People wanna feel better, Lu'.

Lulu   But we can't actually make them better.

Rocco   No – but they think we can. People have Angelato – they feel good. So when they feel bad what do they want? Me, Lulu. Me. (*Beat.*) Jus' cos somethin' seems bad – jus' cos a few people might think it is – never rule out the possibility that it could do an awful lot o' good.

Lulu   Such as?

Rocco (*beat*)   Global warmin'.

Lulu   What's good about that?

Rocco   It's a godsend for ice-cream men: that beautiful little hole in the sky gettin' bigger 'n' bigger day by day. I say, 'Spray those CFCs!' Cos business will *boom* when the people *burn*.

Lulu (*laughs*)   Sometimes I think we're eatin' too much of our own ice cream.

She finishes her cornet. **Rocco** *stares at the Roman stone.*

Rocco   Bet this aint even an actual Roman stone. Be a replica.

Lulu   Reckon?

Rocco   Yeah.

*There is a pause, then **Lulu** stretches her arm out, crooks her finger and beckons **Rocco** towards her.*

Rocco   What's in it for Rocco?

Lulu   You'll see.

Lulu *kisses **Rocco**. He kisses her back. Just as the kiss becomes more passionate again, another train thunders over the viaduct. Immediately, **Lulu** pulls away. **Rocco** leaps up and throws his arms in the air in frustration.*

Lulu   Tell me when. Exactly when.

Rocco   When what?!

Lulu   When you'll leave her.

Rocco   Soon as you leave Lino.

Lulu   If I do leave Lino, you will leave Bernie? You will, honest?

Rocco   How many times do I have to tell you? (*Beat.*) And if it's cryin' you're after, you wait till you tell him – wait till you tell Lino it's all over.

Lulu   Think there'll be tears?

Rocco *drops the Roman stone to the ground.*

Rocco   Enough to drown in.

Three

Early October 1990. Living room of Bernie and Rocco's house.

Bernie *sits in an armchair;* **Lulu** *on the settee. There is an awkward silence. Both sip from coffee cups. Eventually, **Bernie** stops sipping and goes to speak – but either can't think of what to say or how to say it. After a pause, she gives up and resumes sipping the coffee. **Lulu** finishes her coffee and puts her cup down.*

Lulu   Thanks, then.

Bernie   Sorry?

Lulu   Thanks.

Bernie   For?

Lulu   Askin' me round.

Bernie   Oh right. For askin' you round. Right.

Lulu   Makes me feel . . . part o' things . . . the family . . . y'know.

Bernie   Oh, the – (*mimes 'family'*).

Lulu   Yeah.

Bernie   Right. (*Beat.*) Right.

There is another pause, then **Bernie** *puts her cup down as well.* **Lulu** *smiles at her.*

Bernie   We really do need to talk.

Lulu   We are, aren't we?

Bernie   Well, yeah. (*Beat.*) But, you know that . . .

Lulu   What?

Bernie   That . . .

Lulu   *What?*

Bernie   (*beat*)   I think you know.

Lulu   About the business?

Bernie   In a way.

Lulu   About Lino?

Bernie   You do know.

Lulu   Don't see how it matters.

Bernie   It does matter, Lulu.

Lulu   Well, I know it matters, but / I . . .

Bernie   I don't see how you can say it doesn't matter.

Lulu   I didn't. I'm not sayin' that.

Bernie   You did. I heard you – (*mimes 'with my own ears'*).

Lulu   Well I know I said it, but I didn't mean it quite like /
it . . .

Bernie   I'd like to thank you for your hard work over the
last year.

Lulu   You'd like to thank me?

Bernie   On behalf of . . . all of us. We would – we really
would – like to put our thanks on record.

Lulu   It's OK.

Bernie   So that's recorded, then?

Lulu   Well, I'm pleased you're all happy, / I'm . . .

Bernie   We are – oh, we are – but / it's . . .

Lulu   A but?

Bernie   It's a big but. Obviously.

Lulu   This isn't? You're not?

Bernie   We've talked about it – talked about nothin' else
since you and Lino – (*mimes 'split up'*) and we do think it's
time for us to go our separate ways.

Lulu   Who's us?

Bernie   The family. We think / that . . .

Lulu   This isn't about the family. It's about one person.
One person thinks / that . . .

Bernie   No, *we* think – we've discussed it – and we really
do think / that . . .

Lulu   One person. This is one person's idea, isn't it?

Bernie   It may have been one person's idea, but we *all* think
that it would be . . . inappropriate . . . for you to continue

workin' with – and for – (*mimes 'the family'*) given the circumstances. (*Beat.*) D'you understand?

Pause.

Lulu   Where's my cake?

Bernie   Pardon?

Lulu   What about me cake?

Bernie   What cake?

Lulu   You said you were invitin' me round for coffee and cake. We've had the coffee – where's the cake?

Bernie   Well, we haven't got round to the cake.

Lulu   Well, let's get round to it. Come on. Let's get round to the cake. I want the cake.

Bernie   It's probably not the moment for cake now, is it?

Lulu   Is it not?

Bernie   No.

She stands up.

Lulu   You can't sack me.

Bernie   We're not *sacking* you. We'll give you a glowing reference.

Lulu   No, *you* can't sack me.

Bernie   Well it's not *me* – as such – it's / more . . .

Lulu   You don't even work for 'em.

Bernie   I'm *married* to them.

Lulu   You've got nothin' to do with the ice cream.

Bernie   I help out.

Lulu   When do you help out?

Bernie   I *am* helpin' out – (*mimes 'now'*).

Lulu   You're doin' someone else's dirty work.

Bernie (*beat*)   It's *not* a sacking: it's just . . . a natural end . . . the end of a relationship . . . personally *and* professionally.

Lulu   This isn't how you do business.

Bernie   It *is* a family business. This is how *family* business is done.

Lulu (*beat*)   I want . . . my . . . cake.

Rocco *marches in, carrying his briefcase. He is clearly dismayed to see that* **Lulu** *is still there.*

Lulu (*to* **Rocco**)   You won't believe this.

Bernie (*to* **Rocco**)   I've told her.

Rocco   How long does it take, Bernie? Thought she'd've gone by now.

Lulu   She? It's me.

Rocco   I'll come back later.

Bernie   You can stay, Rocco.

Lulu   Yeah, stay.

Bernie   *You* can stay, Lulu's going.

Lulu   No I'm not.

Bernie   Would probably be best.

Rocco   I'll go. It's alright.

Bernie   You don't have to go anywhere – it's your house.

Lulu (*to* **Rocco**)   She says I'm sacked.

Bernie   I didn't actually say that.

Rocco   I will. I'll come back later.

Lulu   Did you know?

Rocco   See you around, Lu'.

Lulu　See me around?

Bernie　I doubt we'll see her around.

Rocco　All the best.

Lulu　*Stay.*

Rocco　And what could possibly be in it for Rocco?

He starts to exit. **Lulu** *stares at him.*

Lulu　I wouldn't go if I were you.

Rocco *stops.*

Lulu　I really wouldn't.

Rocco　Well, you're not me. So . . .

Lulu　I'll . . . I'll . . .

Rocco　You'll what?

Lulu　I will.

Bernie　You'll what?

Rocco　You won't.

Bernie　What won't she?

Lulu　Won't I?

Rocco　We both know you won't.

Bernie　What's going on?

Lulu　This isn't fair.

Rocco　You broke my brother's heart. (*Smiles.*) That wasn't fair either, was it?

Lulu *is stunned.* **Rocco** *turns and exits.*

Lulu　Rocco!

Bernie (*beat*)　Rocco's right, Lulu love: brothers will stick together.

Lulu　What?

Bernie You really should – (*mimes 'go'*). Don't make it any worse than it is.

Lulu (*beat, then slowly*) I came for coffee and cake. I've 'ad my coffee, but I 'aven't 'ad my cake.

Bernie I do honestly think / that . . .

Lulu Who cares?

Bernie What?

Lulu What *you* think? Who cares?

Bernie There's no need / to . . .

Lulu Who are yer at all? What exactly is your position in this family? (*She stands up too.*)

Bernie Lulu . . .

Lulu A second-rate wife to Rocco?

Bernie How dare you.

Lulu Or a second-rate wife to Giuseppe? And a second-rate mam to Lino.

Bernie That's enough.

Lulu Rocco doesn't want yer – and yer know it. That's why he's always at work and you're always with Lino and Giuseppe.

Bernie Get out of my house.

Bernie *moves one way,* **Lulu** *moves the other.*

Lulu I invented Angelato.

Bernie Who did?

Lulu I did.

Bernie Rocco did.

Lulu Me *and* Rocco. We were gonna run the business. Together.

Bernie   You and Rocco?

Lulu   Was gonna happen.

Bernie   Was *never* gonna happen.

Lulu   And jus' coz Lino wants to get rid o' *me*, cos I've got rid of *him*, / he . . .

Bernie   It's not *Lino*. It's *Rocco*.

Lulu   What?

Bernie   It was Rocco's idea. Like I said – brothers will stick together. Rocco asked Giuseppe to sack you. So Giuseppe asked me.

Pause.

Lulu   So sacked, then?

Bernie   Sacked. Yeah.

Lulu   Pardon?

Bernie   You're sacked.

Lulu   I can't – (*mimes 'hear you'*). You'll 'ave to – (*mimes 'speak up'*).

Bernie   You heard me.

Lulu   Nobody hears yer. Nobody listens.

Bernie *steps back, and drops into the seat* **Lulu** *had originally been sitting in.*

Bernie (*whispers*)   Get out . . . of my . . . house.

Lulu   What was that? I can't quite pick it up. You seem to be tryna say somethin'. Mm? Maybe not. (*Beat.*) But there are things I could – (*mimes 'say'*) that'd make you – (*mimes 'listen'*). Even if you'd prefer not to.

Lulu *turns her back on* **Bernie**.

Bernie   Who do you think you are, eh? What do you think you are to this family? You are nothin'. You are nobody.

You slept with a son and that's that. That's it. So get out.
Now.

Lulu Which son?

Pause.

Bernie What?

Lulu You said I slept with a son. 'And that's that.' So I'm
just askin' − in case this gets confusin'. I wanna check. Are
we talkin' about the same son? Hey? (*Beat.*) *Which son?*

Four

A few hours later. Outside **Bernie** *and* **Rocco's** *house.*

Clearly upset, **Lino** *rides down the road at full pelt on his bike, then
flings it to the ground. He rings the door bell of* **Bernie** *and* **Rocco's**
*house. It plays an ice-cream-van-style jingle. There is no answer. He
hammers on the door. A light goes on upstairs.*

Lino (*shouts*) Open the door!

Rocco (*offstage, shouts*) What's in it for Rocco?

Lino Open it!

He looks up as **Rocco** *appears at an upstairs window and opens it.*

Rocco Shut yer mouth − you'll wake the whole street up.

Lino Since when did you care about anybody other than
yourself?

Rocco *laughs.*

Lino Down 'ere. Now.

Rocco What yer gonna do? Beat me up?

Lino Come on.

Rocco Go home to bed. You're embarrassin' yourself.

Lino I know everythin'!

Rocco *looks alarmed.*

Rocco   Whaddya know?

Lino   'Bout you and Lulu.

Rocco *relaxes.*

Rocco   I'm very pleased for you. Can I go now?

Lino   Doin' it to me's one thing – you've always done it to me – but why do it to Bernie?

Rocco   Why I do whatever I do has got nothin' to do with you.

Lino   She's stayin' at Papa's. She won't come back 'ere. How can she ever come back?

Rocco *disappears momentarily, then reappears clutching a heap of Bernie's clothes and throws them out of the window – down towards* **Lino**.

Rocco   Give these to her, then. And tell her I'll paint over the stars.

Rocco *slams the upstairs window shut and the light goes off.*

Lino   We'll take down the swing 'n' all, cos let's face it – it was never gonna be swung!

He rings the door bell again and hammers on the door. A light comes on downstairs, and **Lino** *backs away. The door swings open.* **Rocco** *marches out into the street carrying an armful of toiletries and a bin-bag.* **Lino** *continues to back away, but* **Rocco** *storms straight at him – dumping everything at his feet.*

Rocco   There yer go. That's everythin'.

Lino   How could you do it?

Rocco   Was very easy.

Lino   How?

Rocco   Lulu wanted me, Lino. She wanted a man.

Lino   Bastard!

A light goes upstairs in the house next door. **Rocco** *looks towards it.*

Rocco See? Said you'd wake everyone up. (*To the upstairs light.*) Go back to sleep, love! There's nothin' goin' on!

Lino (*to the upstairs light*) Yeah, there is: me brother's been shaggin' my fiancée!

Rocco Lino!

Lino It's true!

Rocco Forget about her: she's not worth gettin' into a state about.

Lino I loved her.

Rocco There yer go: don't ever make that mistake again.

Lino Did *you*?

Rocco What?

Lino Love her.

Rocco *bursts out laughing and can't stop.*

Rocco Sorry . . . it's just . . . you said that with a dead straight face, but . . . you are takin' the piss, right?

A light goes on upstairs in the house on the other side of **Rocco**'s.

Not another one. (*To both of the upstairs lights.*) Turn your lights out! Turn 'em out!

Lino (*to both of the upstairs lights*) No, keep 'em on! *He runs from one side of the street to the other, shouting up at the windows. To both of the upstairs lights.* Wake up! Everyone! Turn your lights on!

Rocco Shut up!

Lino (*to both of the upstairs lights*) Come on! Lights on!

Lights start to come on all down the street and across the road. **Rocco** *grabs* **Lino**.

Rocco Stop it!

Lino Rocco Raffa.

Rocco What?

Lino Part Lex Luther, part Willy Wonka. Think you're sommat. But you're nowt.

Rocco *pushes* **Lino** *away from him.*

Rocco I'm about to get the one thing I want, and that's more than you. The business is all but mine.

Lino It's not about the business. It's never just been about that. It's not about ice cream. It's about our lives.

Rocco It's the same thing. Don't you see that? Ice cream *is* our life. It's what we're made of.

Lino It's all wrong. Everythin' is wrong.

Rocco You're a casualty, Lino. You're bound to feel that way. (*Beat. To all of the upstairs lights.*) And listen up, all of yer, hidin' behind yer curtains. Cos there's loads like him: tied to the ground, necks broke, throats slit, drowned, drained, and cut into pieces. But come on – don't blame me for tastin' the meat. Cos I say bollocks to what's gone: look at what's left. A finer cut you couldn't get. (*Beat.*) Now is not the time for fastin'. Eat as much as you can!

He takes his wallet from his pocket, opens it, and waves a wad of cash at **Lino**.

Count the money. Count it. Count.

He throws it up into the air, so that it falls down onto him and **Lino**.

Rocco Wear your heart on your wallet, man, cos I did it. I've done it.

Rocco *throws his wallet at* **Lino**.

Lino Bubbles fell on me once.

Rocco Bubbles?

Lino   I thought they'd fall for ever. That as long as they fell – as long as someone cared for *me*, and I cared for *them* – things might never be easy, but they'd always be OK.

Rocco   Whatever.

Lino   The bubbles don't fall any more, Rocco. Won't ever fall again.

Rocco   Why don't you just take her stuff and go?

Lino   You know exactly what you're doin', don't yer? Sort of hoped yer didn't, but yer do.

He picks up the bin-bag and starts to pile **Bernie***'s clothes and toiletries into it – whilst ignoring the money.* **Rocco** *stops ands turns back.*

Rocco   At midnight on Chrimbo Eve – when Bernie starts gettin' dinner ready – yer really expect me to think o' the turkey's feelin's? (*Beat.*) A bird that can't fly deserves slaughterin'.

Lino   You're lost, Rocco. Somehow, sometime, you got lost – and never found your way back.

Rocco   I'm hungrier than you. And I'm not the only one. Learn to taste the meat, Lino. Learn to taste it like me.

Lino   She told me she'd break my heart. But I told her she wouldn't. And she won't. She might be somebody's kryptonite, but she's not mine.

As **Lino** *goes to put the last two objects into the bin-bag – a couple of cans of hairspray –* **Rocco** *snatches them from him and points them at* **Lino** *like guns.*

Rocco   You would love to be Rocco Raffa! (*To all of the upstairs lights.*) You'd all love to be me!

He fires the cans of hairspray up into the air:

(*Shouts.*)   Fuck the ozone!

Clutching the bin-bag, **Lino** *picks up the bike and starts to push it away.*

Rocco   That's it. Get on your bike and ride! And take the money with you – so you can get yourself a nice suit to wear down the Job Centre.

He laughs and starts to fire the cans of hairspray up into the air again as **Lino** *stops and turns:*

Lino   The business won't be mine. But it won't be yours either. (*Beat.*) Papa's sellin' it Rocco. He's sold us all. And all you've done is get him a better price.

Lino *exits.* **Rocco**'*s hands start to shake – the hairspray from the can stuttering and stuttering, till it stops.*

Five

Early November 1990. 'The Hidden Gem', Roman Catholic church, Manchester.

Giuseppe *kneels at the altar. His head is bowed and his hands are together. A choir practises in a back-room, singing 'Ave Maria'. A crucifix hangs above his head whilst, to one side, a number of votive lights are lit.* **Lulu** *enters. She stares at the crucifix, then approaches* **Giuseppe**.

Lulu   Didn't know whether you'd be here or not.

Giuseppe   Kneel.

Lulu *kneels alongside him.* **Giuseppe**'*s eyes remain closed.*

Lulu   Thanks for comin'.

Giuseppe   Bow your head.

Lulu *puts her hands together, closes her eyes and bows her head too.*

Giuseppe   Why here?

Lulu   Never been before.

Giuseppe   You do surprise me.

Lulu   Don't be sarcastic, Giuseppe. We're neither of us angels.

Giuseppe   You've torn my family apart.

Lulu   No. *You* did that.

Giuseppe *spins round for a second – eyes wide open, hands unclasped.*

Giuseppe   Me? Cos of you my home is filled with broken hearts. Lino won't work. Bernie won't talk. And all Rocco does is work and talk – but not to us, cos it's too late. None of gelato he sells now counts for anything.

Lulu   Oh, it counts, Giuseppe. It all counts.

Giuseppe   Within days Raffa's Ices will be sold. And only thing that'll count then is this: I will be rich man.

Lulu *is unmoved.* **Giuseppe** *returns to his original position.*

Giuseppe   So you want to talk about money?

Lulu   No.

Giuseppe   Well you won't be getting pay-off from me. Not penny of compensation after what you've done.

Lulu   I don't want your money.

Giuseppe   And if you've got problem with that, then sue me. I'll see you in court.

Lulu   I want your help.

Giuseppe (*beat*)   *You* want *my* help?

Lulu   Your support.

Giuseppe   I don't know what game you're playing, /
but . . .

Lulu   No game. Not any more.

Giuseppe   So?

Lulu   D'y'ever think about Heaven, Giuseppe? Ever worry that your sins'll find you out?

Giuseppe   I'm God-fearing man.

Lulu   But are you God-loving?

Giuseppe   I sleep well.

Lulu   I don't.

She stands up and walks over to the votive lights.

Can I light one o' these?

Giuseppe   If you have somebody to pray for.

Lulu   There's always someone to pray for. But is there anyone to pray to?

Giuseppe   You pray to Our Lady of Manchester.

Lulu (*beat*)   There aren't any matches.

Giuseppe   I haven't got time for this.

Lulu   Well, what am I meant to use?

Giuseppe   Each candle lights from other. Long as one's lit, you can light lot. (*Beat.*) Now I'm going. I've said what I wanted to say.

He goes to exit. **Lulu** *picks up one of the candles.*

Lulu   The children of Manchester are sick, Giuseppe Raffa. And it's all your fault.

Giuseppe *stops and turns quickly.*

Giuseppe   Pardon?

Lulu   There's a little kid, in the Royal, on a life-support machine.

Giuseppe   And?

Lulu   He overdosed. His parents don't know how. The police don't know how.

Giuseppe   So light light for him. Say prayer.

He waits for an answer. **Lulu** *lights one candle from the other.* **Giuseppe** *shakes his head and goes to exit again.* **Lulu** *lifts the lit candle and speaks softly.*

Lulu   There's coke in the ice cream, y'know.

Giuseppe *stops once more – but this time he turns very slowly.*

Lulu   We've been puttin' cocaine in the mix. That's what Angelato is.

Giuseppe (*beat*)   You're lying.

Lulu   I made it first. But it was never meant to be for sale – was just for me. (*Beat.*) Then Rocco tasted it. (*Beat.*) He wanted to win so bad. And it tasted so good. Seemed funny at first – and when it started to sell . . . (*Beat.*) but now I've not got nothin' – and no one – and that kid's in hospital – and it doesn't seem funny any more.

Giuseppe   Please tell me you're lying.

Lulu   A little bit makes such a lot o' difference. Makes the ice cream taste *so* . . . ice-creamy.

Giuseppe   Oh . . .

Lulu   People can't get enough o' the stuff. They want it without hardly knowin' why. Eat it, and they're the life and soul. But half an hour later when things are back to normal, it's more ice cream they want. And only Angelato'll do.

Giuseppe   How could you?

Lulu   We did it for you. Did it to win. There might've been a time when ice cream on its own was enough – when ice cream was everything – but that's gone. (*Beat.*) People wanted more. So we gave 'em more.

Giuseppe   They didn't want more! They wanted what they'd always had. But cos you couldn't give it to them, you made them believe they needed something else.

Lulu   Rocco can't stop. He's out o' control. (*Beat.*) I'm gonna go to the police. I've got to.

Giuseppe   What can police do?

Lulu   They need to know.

Giuseppe   *No one* needs to know. I can sort it.

Lulu   It's too late.

Giuseppe   Leave it to me.

Lulu   It's too big for you. For all of us.

Giuseppe   We'll destroy all Angelato. Pretend nothing ever happened.

Lulu   But something *has* happened.

Giuseppe   You can't go to police. I'm about to sell everything. I'm about to sell it all. (*Beat.*) You can have cut of it. You can have piece.

Lulu *puts the candle down.*

Giuseppe   Well?

Lulu   When we was kids, me 'n' me brother got home from school once and could smell smoke. Comin' from the back yard.

Giuseppe   Take money, Lulu.

Lulu   Me dad always used to have his rollies out there, and we thought, 'he's come home.'

Giuseppe   Take it.

Lulu   So we ran out, and there was all these ashes. And in the ashes, money.

Giuseppe   Money?

Lulu   Most I'd ever seen. Great big pile o' coins. No notes. Guess the more it's worth, the quicker it burns.

Giuseppe   Whose was it?

Lulu   Me dad's. When he went and he wa'n't comin' back, he left it with a note – 'for the children'. For me. And Joe. But me mam di'n't want us to have it. Di'n't want anythin' *from* him, or *left* of him / and . . .

Giuseppe   She burnt the money?

Lulu   And I thought – I've gotta have it – can all be mine. And no one'll know but Joe.

Giuseppe   You took it?

Lulu   Grabbed two great handfuls of it. Overflowin'.

Giuseppe   And?

Lulu *tugs at the index finger of one of her hands and starts to slowly take her gloves off.*

Lulu   Joe shouted at me not to. Like hot coals, see. Coppers and fives, tens and fifties. All over me 'ands like leeches. Hurt so much I cou'n't scream. Burnt so bad I cou'n't speak.

She drops her gloves, and grips **Giuseppe***'s face with her hands.*

Lulu   I grabbed Joe. Grabbed his face. Wanted him to help me. To make it go away. But I jus burnt him too.

Giuseppe *takes* **Lulu***'s hands from his face and studies them.*

Giuseppe   Royalty all over your palms.

Lulu   They had to chip 'em off later. Off both of us.

Giuseppe   They're almost beautiful.

Lulu   I've always hated 'em – but I'm not gonna wear my gloves any more.

Giuseppe   You shouldn't. (*Beat.*) Rocco is no longer Raffa, Lulu. He's dead to me. And Lino? Bernie? Not my problem anymore. But you can have whatever you want. I'll give you everything I've got.

Lulu   I don't want your money, Giuseppe. I want to save the children. All the little children. (*Beat.*) I want to – and I'm goin' to.

Giuseppe   Fuck children – what about me?!

As **Giuseppe** *lets go of* **Lulu***'s hands, he suddenly remembers where he is and looks around him – but the choir continues to rehearse.*

Giuseppe   You're throwing me to lions here.

Lulu *bows her head in front of the votive lights.* **Giuseppe** *points to one side.*

Giuseppe   If you want to confess, go in there.

Lulu   That's not enough.

Giuseppe   It'll make things better.

Lulu   For who?

Giuseppe   For you.

Lulu   And what about everybody else? (*Beat.*) I didn't even light that candle for the little boy. My prayer, Giuseppe, was for you.

Giuseppe   I don't want you to pray for me.

Lulu   I prayed to Our Lady of Manchester.

Giuseppe   Don't want candle lit for me!

He marches over to the votive lights and blows out the one that **Lulu** *lit.*

Lulu   Come with me. That's what I'm here for. What I'm askin'. Let's do it right. Come with me, Papa. We'll go together.

Giuseppe (*beat*)   You'll destroy us all.

Lulu *shakes her head and goes to exit.* **Giuseppe** *grabs her shoulder, but she shakes him off and exits quickly. The singing of the choir grows louder and louder.* **Giuseppe** *walks back over to the votive lights and pauses for a moment, before blowing out each and every candle in turn, till there are no lights left.*

Six

The next day. Production area of Raffa's ice-cream factory.

Bernie *enters and looks around her.* **Rocco***'s briefcase is on the floor.*

Bernie   Hello? (*Beat.*) Hello?

She walks round the mixing machine. There is no sign of anybody. She walks round the pasteurisation tanks and frowns as she smells gas. There is still no sign of anybody. She walks round the holding tank, then lifts its lid. At the very moment she does so, a man roars and leaps out – holding a gun and sending ice cream showering all around him. **Bernie** *screams and staggers back, then turns to see* **Rocco** *standing there – air rifle poised – shivering, gasping for breath, and covered head to foot in ice cream. They stare at each other, panting.*

Rocco (*pants*)   Bloody 'ell, Bernie!

Bernie (*pants*)   You made me – (*mimes 'jump'*)

Rocco   Thought you were the coppers. (*Pants.*) They're after me.

Bernie (*pants*)   I know.

Rocco   Yer do?

Bernie   They've arrested Giuseppe and Lino, but it's you they want.

Rocco   She's tryna destroy everythin' we've got.

Bernie   That little boy's still on the life-support machine and I *hate* you for it.

Rocco   What little boy?

Bernie   It's too late for that, Rocco.

Rocco   I don't know what you're talkin' about.

Bernie   I wish to God you didn't. But you do.

Rocco   We can't let her do this to us. We're too strong for her.

Bernie *We?*

Dripping, **Rocco** *drops his gun, staggers over to the wall and grabs a bucket and two mops. He hands one of the mops to* **Bernie**. *She just stares at him.*

Rocco You do that side. I'll do this. (*Beat.*) Make sure you don't leave a trace of anything.

Bernie I'm not − (*mimes 'mopping'*).

Rocco Why not?

Bernie *Why not?*

She throws the mop at **Rocco**.

Bernie After what you've done?

Rocco I'm the victim.

Bernie *You?*

Rocco Been tricked and conned and blackmailed and set up.

Bernie Forget it, Rocco.

Rocco Forget what?

Bernie Think I came lookin' for you to see how you are? To give you a hand? I'm here to tell you to give yourself up. To tell the truth for once in your life: tell the police that it's got nothing' to do with Giuseppe and Lino.

Rocco I am telling the truth, Bern, I am. So please help me.

Bernie Why would I possibly help you now?

Rocco I need you. Always have.

Bernie Liar.

Rocco I love you.

Bernie No you don't.

Rocco I married you.

Bernie   Long time ago.

Rocco   You have to believe me. Believe in me, Bernie.
Believe.

Bernie   I don't – (*mimes 'believe'*). How can I? And I
haven't even got the energy to protest about it any more.

Rocco *moves towards* **Bernie**. *She moves away from him.*

Bernie   Don't come near me. Don't touch me.

Rocco   But Bernie, / I . . .

Bernie   Don't!

Pause.

Rocco   Was just sex.

Bernie   What?

Rocco   I was drunk – and told her it was a mistake. Felt
awful about it. But she starts sayin', 'Mistake? Fuck you
mistake!' Went all Glenn Close on me. Threatenin' me: 'If
yer don't do this, I'll do that.' And I was scared. Ashamed.
Didn't want anyone to find out. Or get hurt.

Bernie   No, Rocco. You think I'm – (*mimes 'an idiot'*) but
I'm not.

Rocco   I swear to you. She said that I had to give her a
job when I took over the business. And I went along with it.
I'm not proud of it, but I did. Till she dumped Lino. And
I couldn't take it any more. I thought, 'She's gotta go,' even
if we all get hurt in the process.

Bernie   And the rest?

Rocco   The rest?

Bernie   The ice cream! Angelato!

Rocco   What about it?

Bernie   The cocaine!

Rocco   Cocaine? This is an ice-cream factory.

Bernie   The police'll come here, Rocco. They'll knock that door down and search this place.

Rocco   Look around you. Where could I hide it in 'ere?

Bernie   So why d'you need to clean up? Why don't you want to leave a trace of anything?

Rocco   It's not the coppers I'm worried about – it's the Environmental Health. They're bound to get involved. And look at this place. Smell it.

Bernie   The gas hit me as soon as I walked in. That tank still need fixing?

Rocco   *Everythin'* needs fixin'. And they'd want the whole factory pulled down.

Pause.

Bernie   What is in Angelato?

Rocco   Stuff that maybe there shouldn't be. Flavour enhancers. Additives. Shedload o' sugar. That's why it tastes as good as it does. (*Beat.*) But cocaine? A kid on a life-support machine? I really don't know what you're talkin' about. All I'm guilty of is rottin' a few teeth. And I'm an ice cream man. That's my job.

Rocco *moves towards* **Bernie** *again. This time she doesn't move away.*

Bernie   Do you promise me?

Rocco   Yeah, I promise. I *swear* to yer. This is so important. Trust me. This is absolutely one-hundred-per-cent truth. Cross my heart and hope to die.

He runs his finger down **Bernie**'s *face, leaving ice cream dribbling down her cheek.*

Bernie   Then you've really got to go to the police.

Rocco   I will. Just help me get rid of all the ice cream first. All I wanted was Raffa's ices to be all Rocco's. And it aint gonna be. Ever. It's about to be sold. So let's leave it right, eh. Let's leave it nice.

Bernie (*quietly*)   But what's in it for Bernie?

Rocco (*mimes 'my heart, my heart'*)   That's what.

Bernie *nods.* **Rocco** *picks up her mop.* **Bernie** *sniffs the air again, frowns once more, then takes the mop from him. Both start to mop quickly. Suddenly, there is a loud bang outside on one of the corrugated walls of the factory, followed by a fluttering of wings.* **Bernie** *spins around.* **Rocco** *drops his bucket. After a pause, there is another bang at the opposite side of them, followed by another fluttering of wings. They turn to face back that way. The banging continues from both sides.* **Rocco** *picks up his gun, runs and jumps back into the holding tank. He takes a deep breath, then disappears into it – pulling the lid shut behind him. There is a shout from outside.*

Boy 1 (*offstage*)   Ice cream!

Bernie *looks in the direction of the shout. Then there is another one.*

Girl 1 (*offstage*)   Ice cream!

Bernie *looks around her, then runs over to the holding tank, lifts the lid up and plunges her hands into the ice cream.*

Boy 1 (*offstage*)   Ice cream!

She hauls **Rocco***'s head out. He gasps and tries to go back under, but she pulls him out again.*

Rocco   Let go!

Bernie   It's not the police. It's kids.

Rocco   *Kids?*

The banging continues from both sides – then a third side as well.

Boy 1 (*offstage*)   Ice cream!

Bernie   They want ice cream.

Girl 1 (*offstage*)   Ice cream!

Rocco   I'll kill the little bastards.

Boy 2 (*offstage*)   Ice cream!

Bernie   They're desperate, Rocco.

The ice cream drips from **Rocco** *as he clambers back out of the tank and clicks the barrel of the rifle into place.*

Bernie   You can't shoot them!

Boy (*offstage*)   Ice cream!

Rocco   Watch me.

Girl 1 (*offstage*)   Ice cream!

Bernie   You might kill them!

Boy 2 (*offstage*)   Ice cream!

Rocco   It's just an air rifle: only be surface wounds, but'll soon shut 'em up.

Bernie *runs and stands in front of* **Rocco**. *Just as he goes to push her out of his way, more banging is heard: this time from the roof. The manic flapping of wings up above gets worse.*

Girl 2 (*offstage*)   Ice cream!

Rocco   How many of 'em are there?

Bernie   *Why* are they so desperate?

The banging on the walls continues along with the flight of the departing birds. The chant becomes a mantra and more and more children's voices are heard.

Children (*offstage, in unison*)   Ice cream! Ice cream! Ice cream!

Bernie   What're we gonna do?

Rocco   Ignore 'em. They'll go away.

Bernie   What if they smash the windows?

Rocco   Why would they?

Bernie   What if they set fire to the factory?

Rocco   They won't.

Bernie   But the gas . . .

Children (*offstage, in unison*)   Ice cream! Ice cream! Ice cream!

There is a pause, then **Bernie** *runs past* **Rocco**.

Rocco   Where are you goin'?

Bernie   To turn the air-con on.

Rocco   Don't do that.

Bernie   It – (*mimes 'smells'*) really strong.

Rocco   But it's never used!

Bernie   If they – (*mimes 'light a match'*) . . .

Rocco   *Don't!*

Children (*offstage, in unison*)   Ice cream! Ice cream! Ice cream!

Bernie *ignores* **Rocco**, *opens the box on the wall, and flicks a switch. The sound of air blowing adds to the banging, chanting and flapping.* **Rocco** *drops to his knees.*

Bernie   It's gonna be alright, Rocco. Think I believe in you again.

A fine white powder starts to fall from the ceiling, blowing out of the air-conditioning unit. **Rocco** *stares down at the ground.* **Bernie** *looks up. The powder fills the air, covering everything.*

Children (*offstage, in unison*)   Ice cream! Ice cream! Ice cream!

Bernie   Rocco? (*Beat.*) Rocco?

Rocco   They used to put Coca in the Cola, Bern – so we put it in the cone.

Bernie *stares up at the falling powder in horror as* **Rocco** *reaches out to her with his arms.*

Rocco   You have to forgive me. Cos I need you now. I really do.

Children (*offstage, in unison*)   Ice cream! Ice cream! Ice cream!

Rocco　You know you can't leave me.

Children (*offstage, in unison*)　Ice cream! Ice cream! Ice cream!

Rocco　I'm everythin' to you.

Children (*offstage, in unison*)　Ice cream! Ice cream! Ice cream!

Rocco　You won't. (*Beat.*) Don't.

Bernie *stares at* **Rocco** *and shuffles backwards as a cocaine cloud descends on them both.*

Bernie *mimes 'I . . . loved you . . . But you . . . have ripped . . . my heart out. Have ripped . . . all . . . our hearts out!'.*

The flapping of wings ends as the last bird flies away. **Rocco** *closes his eyes and starts to cry.*

Rocco　Make 'em stop. Make 'em go away.

Children (*offstage, in unison*)　Ice cream! Ice cream! Ice cream!

Rocco　Please.

All of a sudden, there is the sound of a police siren. The banging and chanting stops immediately as the children scarper. A blue light flashes from outside the front of the factory.

Bernie *mimes 'It's over.' She reaches inside her pocket, takes out a feather, and backs even further away from* **Rocco**. *He jumps up, runs and grabs his briefcase, and goes to exit. As he does so, his case falls open and a dozen bricks fall from it. He pauses, then flings the case to the floor, runs to the back of the factory, and finally exits.* **Bernie** *looks at the bricks, then the feather, and turns towards the blue flashing light.*

Seven

Late November 1990. Production area of Raffa's ice-cream factory.

Heavy rain beats down upon the battered frame of the factory. Inside, police tape weaves around everything. **Giuseppe** *enters and looks around him. He is soaked through to the skin. His hair – normally* *immaculate – is plastered limply to his forehead. He steps over the police tape and shuffles towards the pasteurisation tank. He takes one of the votive lights from his pocket, then leans on the side of the side of the tank – staring at the unlit candle in his hands.* **Lino** *enters.*

Lino   Papa?

Without turning to face **Lino**, **Giuseppe** *drops the candle onto the floor.* **Lino** *moves towards the candle and looks at it.*

Giuseppe   Can we light candle for Maria and sing 'Happy Birthday'? Even though she isn't here.

Lino   Don't light anythin'. Not with the gas.

Giuseppe   Today is day. End of competition. Winner declared. So how come we're all losers?

Lino   You're soakin'.

He takes one of the traditional ice-cream-man's jackets from the hook on the wall and goes to put it on **Giuseppe**, *but* **Giuseppe** *shrugs it off and turns round.*

Giuseppe   Not wearin' that.

Lino   You'll catch your death.

Giuseppe   Why should I wear ice-cream man's jacket? When I'm not one.

Lino   You are.

Giuseppe   No.

Lino   You own an ice-cream business.

Giuseppe   *Non ho niente: no ho soldi*; no biz; no gelato.

Lino   What's this then?

Giuseppe   Worthless.

Lino   Isn't.

Giuseppe   If no one wants to buy something, it must be worthless.

Lino I disagree.

Lino *hands* **Giuseppe** *the jacket again, but* **Giuseppe** *throws it to the ground.*

Giuseppe Televisione? Newspapers? Everybody saw?

Lino We don't know that.

Giuseppe Raffa's van – driving wrong way down fast lane of motorway – chased by police cars, cameras and helicopter?

Lino It's Rocco who's ruined.

Giuseppe Doesn't just have his name on van: has all of ours.

Lino But *we* haven't been charged. People'll see that.

Giuseppe Even in days when I had nothing, I had my name.

Lino So why did you try and sell it?

Giuseppe (*beat*) I couldn't even give it away now. Does that make you happy?

Another drip drops down from the roof. **Giuseppe** *and* **Lino** *watch it fall.*

Lino That's not comin' from the roof. I've fixed the leak. And the air-con too. Washed it down and cleaned it up. With soap and water.

One more drip falls. **Giuseppe** *holds his hand out and catches it.*

Giuseppe Is not enough, Merlino. Is not enough. (*Beat.*) Leave me. Go.

There is a pause, then **Lino** *turns and exits.* **Giuseppe** *watches him go, before shuffling over to where the votive light lies on the floor and dropping to his knees. He pulls out a box of matches from his pocket, then takes a deep breath and strikes one. Nothing happens. He strikes it again, but once more it fails to ingite. He throws it to the ground, then tries another match – and when that doesn't work, he pulls out another, and another.* **Lino** *enters again. He pauses for a moment, then – realising what* **Giuseppe** *is doing – runs over to*

him and grabs his hands. They wrestle for a few seconds, till **Lino**
manages to grab the box of matches from **Giuseppe**.

Giuseppe   Matches are all wet. Tipico.

Lino   If you'd've lit that . . .

Giuseppe   Whole place is falling down. If it went up, do
us all favour.

Lino   With you in it?! With me?!

Giuseppe   Thought you'd gone.

Lino   I can't ever go! Don't you see? Ice cream's in my
blood too.

Giuseppe   I asked you to go. Told you to. Why / didn't . . .

Lino *claps his hands together twice.*

Lino   You think it's all about you. But it's not. The ice
cream ain't yours. Never was.

Giuseppe   Then whose it is?

Lino   Everybody's!

Giuseppe *closes his eyes, and then rubs his temples, his hands
trembling.*

Lino   Open your eyes.

Giuseppe   No.

Lino   Open them!

Giuseppe *opens his eyes and looks up above him:*

Giuseppe   *O Maria, sei l'unica persona che mi capisce.*

Lino   *Ti capisco meglio che sai Papa.*

Lino *crouches down onto his knees, alongside* **Giuseppe**.

Giuseppe   We'd never been huggers. But at very end, we
hugged. And hugged. Till I was just hugging her and she
wasn't hugging back. She'd gone. And I put her down. But
how do you go on?

Lino   I miss Mamma too. More than ever on days like this. I want her to be here. But I want you too. (*Beat.*) We're all missin' those who aren't here, Papa. But why are we missin' those who are?

He takes **Giuseppe**'s *arms and both stand up, before stepping away from each other.*

Giuseppe   First time I ever picked you up, you slipped my grip. Everybody gasped – but you just pitter-pattered down, light as feather. And I caught you again. Before you hit ground. But for that half-second you were in air. Unsupported. (*Beat.*) And I called you Merlino – Little Blackbird – but never had confidence to hold you again. Never thought I could.

Lino   You could hold me now.

Giuseppe   How can I? I sunk your ship. And expected you to learn to swim.

Lino   I've nothin' against anybody learnin' to swim', Papa. I jus' don't reckon those that can't should be left to drown.

Giuseppe   Nonno Raffa never learnt.

Lino   He must've. He saved himself.

Giuseppe   He'd never leave shallow end in Victoria Baths, so how could he survive in Atlantic Ocean? Somebody must've kept him afloat.

Lino (*beat*)   If you hold me, I'll hold you.

Giuseppe   I tried to sell our name.

Lino   We're gonna get it back.

Giuseppe   You can't.

Lino   No – I can't . . . but *we* can. (*Beat.*) When I started to fight, I thought I could fight on my own. But I can't. I need you.

Giuseppe   You want *me* to work for *you*?

Lino   No, I want you to work *with* me. And I want Bernie too.

Giuseppe   Bernadette?

Lino   She's walked away from Rocco – not us. She's always wanted to help. And we need help. She can do what I can't. And you can do what we can't.

Giuseppe   It won't work. It won't.

Lino   We are all in this together, Papa. That's all I know.

Giuseppe   D'you have any idea how much money Rocco spent? How much we owe?

Lino *pulls match after match out of the box, before holding one up.*

Lino   This match is dry. If you want the easy way out, take it. But you'll have to take me with you. (*Beat.*) If you still don't believe in me, strike it now, and put us both out of our misery.

He hands **Giuseppe** *both the match and the box, then stands back.* **Giuseppe** *looks around the factory, then at* **Lino**, *then at the match. Outside, there is a pause in the rain.* **Giuseppe** *goes to strike the match, but hesitates. The flapping of wings is heard above as a bird returns to nest on the roof.* **Giuseppe** *makes another attempt to strike the match – but just as he looks like he's really going to do it, he drops it instead.*

Giuseppe   Merlino. *Mi figlio. Mi bellissimo bambino.*

Lino   That boy – in hospital – Bernie says he's gettin' better. He's gonna be alright.

Giuseppe (*beat*)   People of Manchester used to love our gelato. In days before they ate it through cocainomania, they ate it through choice. Didn't give them confidence or energy, or make them think they were comico . . . just tasted good.

Lino   And it still does. Still the best. You can tell people what to eat – what they need, or ought to want – but in the end only they really know.

Giuseppe   Oh, and they knew.

Lino   They *know*.

The flapping of wings above grows louder as all the birds start to return to their nest.

Lino   Birds are back. They're nestin' again.

Giuseppe *picks up the jacket that he threw to the floor, then moves back towards* **Lino** *and holds it up for him.*

Giuseppe   You wear it now. You wear it for me.

Lino *puts the ice-cream-man's jacket on.* **Giuseppe** *straightens the collar on* **Lino**'s *jacket, then smells the gas again. Both he and* **Lino** *sniff the air, then* **Lino** *walks over to the wall, opens the hatch and turns the air-conditioning on. Air blows down from the ceiling.*

Giuseppe   I built this place. Now, I think, it needs rebuilding.

Lino   No, just repairin'. (*Beat.*) I've fixed the roof and the air-conditionin'. I'll fix the tanks too. And when the gas is gone, we'll be able to light as many candles in here as we want.

Giuseppe *crouches down and picks up a stone in one hand and the candle in the other. A soap bubble falls from the air-conditioning unit and floats down to the factory floor without either of them noticing.*

Giuseppe   I'm missing Maria on her birthday -- when I forgot about you on yours.

He wipes his eyes and tries not to cry.

Lino   Go ahead, Papa. Cry. Even the Iron Lady's doin' it. We're all criers now.

Giuseppe *hands the candle to* **Lino**.

Giuseppe   I've always wanted to hold you.

Lino   I've always wanted you to hold me.

Giuseppe   Just don't know if I can.

Lino You can.

Giuseppe What if I drop you again?

Lino Catch me.

Giuseppe But I'm wet. I'll make you wet.

Lino I'm dry. I'll dry you.

The bubble has been followed by other bubbles: at first a dozen or so, then many more. **Giuseppe** *puts the stone in his pocket, and* **Lino** *puts the candle in his.* **Giuseppe** *places his hands on* **Lino***'s face, then his shoulders, and finally his back – before pulling him to him. They hug. The bubbles fall down onto them – hundreds turning into thousands as they fill the air.* **Giuseppe** *buries his head into* **Lino***'s shoulder as the flapping of wings gets louder and louder.* **Lino** *looks up – sees the bubbles – and smiles.*

Giuseppe What do we do now?

Lino (*beat*) Let's make ice cream.

9 780413 775511